PROOF

PROOF

The Book of Mormon and the Second Coming

JAMES R. TATE

Printed in the United States of America.
ISBN: 978-1-63385-481-9
Library of Congress Control Number: 2022922003

Published by
Word Association Publishers
205 Fifth Avenue
Tarentum, Pennsylvania 15084

www.wordassociation.com
1.800.827.7903

With many thanks to my daughters,
Devon Millward and Virginia Isaacson for their help and
encouragement. I am also grateful for those who have
assisted in editing, including particularly Carolyn Ingersoll,
Steve Studdert, Kent Merrell, and Devn Cornish who went
the extra mile to make *Proof* better.

Dedication

This book is dedicated to all people who love our Lord and Savior, Jesus Christ, and look forward to His return in great glory. I am especially mindful of the great people of the South in the United States, among whom I served as a Mission President for The Church of Jesus Christ of Latter-day Saints. A former General Authority of The Church of Jesus Christ of Latter-day Saints, Elder Vaughn J. Featherstone, served in the South and learned to love the people there. Elder Featherstone made this statement while speaking to missionaries called to serve in the Southern States:

President Spencer W. Kimball stated — "Make no small plans: They have no magic to stir men's souls." This is the vision I have for the South. I believe that one day the South will baptize more people into the church than all other English speaking missions in the world together. There are great hosts of marvelous Baptists, members of the Church of Christ, Methodists, and Catholics who are honorable people, and have faith in the Lord Jesus Christ and love him. As they see (their) church veering off to the right or to the left of those basic teachings, they will begin to search for the truth. And as pivotal teachers come into the church and have influence, we will see the time when we will baptize hundreds and thousands, tens of thousands. In your day you will see a million members of the church in the South. There will be Temples Plural in the South States. What a Great call you have to serve with these marvelous people.

(Vaughn J Featherstone, April 30, 1984)

Acknowledgment

The time has arrived for people, who believe in God and trust Him, to come together. A unity of believers concerning issues that really matter can make a positive influence in the direction the World is heading. We must get ready to receive our Lord and Savior, Jesus Christ, in great glory and power. To achieve unity members of different faith groups and denominations must focus on the issues that unite us, not issues that divide us. When we find common ground, we can change the World for the better.

An example of an organization that understands the principle of finding common ground on important matters is the American Family Association headquartered in Tupelo, Mississippi. There is no more important issue than that of preserving the family and the sanctity of marriage. In November 2008 I received an email from Don Wildmon, founder of the American Family Association. Rev. Wildmon attached a petition to his email, signed by many believers of several Christian faiths, thanking President Thomas S. Monson for the contribution that The Church of Jesus Christ of Latter-day Saints made to passing Proposition 8 in California. Proposition 8 was an effort to enshrine traditional marriage between a man and a woman in the California Constitution. In 2008 I was serving as President of the Alabama Birmingham Mission, which included Tupelo, and Rev. Wildmon wanted me to send Thomas S. Monson, then President of The Church of Jesus Christ of

Latter-day Saints, the petition signed by American Family Association members.

I made sure that President Monson received the petition and reflected on Rev. Wildmon's willingness to reach out to The Church of Jesus Christ of Latter-day Saints. Rev. Wildmon had the courage to step out in front and lead the way for Christian unity. The American Family Association's efforts in support of traditional marriage and the traditional family are directly in line with The Proclamation on the Family, published by The Church of Jesus Christ of Latter-day Saints in March 1995. Rev. Wildmon clearly saw common ground and initiated the contact to bring us together. The World is in a rough place, and we need to put aside our differences, as Don Wildmon did, and march together in our Lord's cause.

Contents

Chapter One

Reading The Book of Mormon, Another Testament of Jesus Christ

The Book of Mormon is the Word of God. It contains messages from our Savior and prophets of the Lord. At a minimum we should read what the Lord and his prophets have to say to us.

We don't want to be like the Israelites led by Moses who refused to look up at the brazen serpent - when just looking would have saved them after being bitten by poisonous snakes. The Lord has given us the Book of Mormon as proof that our Heavenly Father is preparing once again to send His Son to the Earth, this time in power and great glory. Bringing forth the Book of Mormon came at the price of some of the best blood of the Nineteenth Century. We need to read it and learn from it.

While serving as President of the Alabama Birmingham Mission of The Church of Jesus Christ of Latter-day Saints, I often had occasion to travel to Huntsville for conferences and to meet with missionaries. Our custom when we needed to spend a few days in Huntsville was to stay at the Marriott Residence Inn. One evening as we prepared for a fireside given by a visiting Church leader, I opened a dresser drawer in our room and saw a Book of Mormon. I immediately had the thought: *I wonder if the manager of this hotel has ever read the Book of Mormon. He probably has over a hundred copies in his hotel.* I decided to meet the manager and find out.

Early the next morning I took a Book of Mormon we'd brought with us and went in to see the hotel manager. He was a nice fellow and asked how we were enjoying our stay at the Residence Inn. I told him that I loved the Residence Inns, and in fact a couple of years previous had stayed for 40 nights at a Residence Inn while trying a case in Reno, Nevada. I then got to the question I wanted to ask: "How many rooms do you have in this hotel?" He answered: "I believe we have 150 rooms." I asked: "Do you have a Book of Mormon in every room?" He answered: "Yes, I believe we do." I asked: "Have you ever read it?" He answered: "No, but I have a Bible right by my bed, and I read it every night."

At that point I asked him if he had a Bible in his office – which he did. I asked him to turn to the Book of Acts in the New Testament and to look at verses 6 and 7 in Acts, Chapter 1. Verses 6 and 7 in the King James Version read:

> *6 When they therefore were come together, they asked of him, saying, Lord, wilt thou at this time restore again the kingdom to Israel?*
>
> *7 And he said unto them, It is not for you to know the times or the seasons, which the Father hath put in his own power.*

I reminded the manager that these two verses were describing what happened just before Jesus ascended into Heaven. His disciples were trying to find out when the Lord would return to the Earth and establish His Kingdom. The Lord explained that the Father would determine the time when He sent His Son back to Earth.

I handed the manager the copy of the Book of Mormon we'd brought and asked him to turn to verse 17 in Chapter 4 of the Book of Ether. Ether is the next to last division in the Book of Mormon; and was written by an ancient prophet who lived in the Americas. He read:

17 Therefore, when ye shall receive this record ye may know that the work of the Father has commenced upon all the face of the land.

I told him that the Book of Mormon was hidden until its publication in 1830 and it was only in our time becoming generally available to people. The Lord did not tell His early disciples when He would return; but He did give them a clue: The Father would decide the time of the Second Coming of our Lord. Here is the Book of Mormon, plainly stating that the work of the Father has commenced. I have included Chapter 4 of Ether in the Book of Mormon in **NOTE 1** (page 193) of the *Appendix* to put verse 17 in context. After we read the scriptures together, I asked the manager if he would read the Book of Mormon. He seemed genuinely interested in learning about proof that our Heavenly Father was preparing once again to send His Son to Earth – this time in power and great glory. I told him to keep the copy I gave him, since I did not want to give him one of his own copies.

In Chapter 4 of Ether, we find verses that seem to say that Jesus Christ and our Heavenly Father are one and the same. It is true that they are one in purpose, just as we are commanded to be one in purpose with the Savior; but they are not the same beings. When Jesus was on the cross, He did not pray to himself. Nor was Jesus trying to deceive His disciples as recorded in Acts 1:7, when He told them that the Father kept the time of His return in the Father's own power. Many people who love the Lord and have studied the Bible do not understand that Jesus and our Heavenly Father are separate beings. I did not realize how widespread this misunderstanding was until I participated with missionaries in discussions with leaders of churches and other leading citizens that lived within the boundaries of the Alabama Birmingham Mission.

It is my practice when possible as part of an introductory Gospel discussion to meet at one of our chapels and explain the paintings that adorn the halls. Chapels of The Church of Jesus Christ of Latter-day Saints are plain and simple, but they do have artwork that illustrate events of the Restoration and key principles of the Gospel of Jesus Christ. I recall on one occasion we were having a first discussion in one of our chapels with a faith leader of another church and his wife. After the lesson, we took a walking tour of our chapel and stopped at several of the paintings where we explained the principle or event depicted. When we reached the large painting in the entrance foyer depicting what Latter-day Saints call "The First Vision", I recited the words of Joseph Smith explaining what he saw. I said the words very slowly, helping to give the Spirit of the Lord time to bear witness of the truth of the words I was speaking:

> *I saw a pillar of light exactly over my head, above the brightness of the sun, which descended gradually until it fell upon me. When the light rested upon me I saw two Personages, whose brightness and glory defy all description, standing above me in the air. One of them spake unto me, calling me by name and said, pointing to the other— Joseph, this is My Beloved Son. Hear Him.*

As I recited the words of the First Vision, I noticed the faith leader's wife staring at the painting, which shows the young boy, Joseph Smith, kneeling in the woods looking up at our Heavenly Father *and* Jesus Christ. I said to her: "Is something wrong?" She answered repeating over and over: "I never knew there were two of them. I never knew there were two of them." Her revelation made a great impression on me. Up to that point I had never realized how widespread must be the misconception that Jesus Christ and our Heavenly Father are the same being. That lack of understanding has prevented many of us from realizing who we really are and understanding our true potential. We human beings are literally sons and daughters of God. Just making that statement can get you killed even today in some parts of the world.

In the New Testament we have a record of the Apostle Paul trying to explain the principle of man's true nature to the Athenians [1.]. We also have a similar explanation in one of Paul's letters [2.]. During his mortal ministry the Lord was almost stoned to death for trying to teach the same principle to religious leaders [3.]. Here are the Biblical references:

1. Paul teaching the Athenians -
   Acts 17:

   *22 ¶ Then Paul stood in the midst of Mars' hill, and said, Ye men of Athens, I perceive that in all things ye are too super-stitious. 23 For as I passed by, and beheld your devotions, I found an altar with this inscription, TO THE UNKNOWN GOD. Whom therefore ye ignorantly worship, him declare I unto you. 24 God that made the world and all things there-in, seeing that he is Lord of heaven and earth, dwelleth not in temples made with hands; 25 Neither is worshipped with men's hands, as though he needed any thing, seeing he giveth to all life, and breath, and all things; 26 And hath made of one blood all nations of men for to dwell on all the face of the earth, and hath determined the times before appointed, and the bounds of their habitation; 27 That they should seek the Lord, if haply they might feel after him, and find him, though he be not far from every one of us: 28 For in him we live, and move, and have our being; as certain also of your own po-ets have said, **For we are also his offspring. 29 Forasmuch then as we are the offspring of God,** we ought not to think that the Godhead is like unto gold, or silver, or stone, graven by art and man's device. 30 And the times of this ignorance God winked at; but now commandeth all men every where to repent: 31 Because he hath appointed a day, in the which he will judge the world in righteousness by that man whom he hath ordained; whereof he hath given assurance unto all men, in that he hath raised him from the dead. 32 ¶ And when they heard of the resurrection of the dead, some mocked: and others said, We will hear thee again of this matter. 33 So Paul departed from among them.* (Emphasis Added).

2. Paul's Letter to the Romans -

Romans 8:

14 For as many as are led by the Spirit of God, they are the sons of God. 15 For ye have not received the spirit of bondage again to fear; but ye have received the Spirit of adoption, whereby we cry, Abba, Father. **16 The Spirit itself beareth witness with our spirit, that we are the children of God: 17 And if children, then heirs; heirs of God, and joint-heirs with Christ;** *if so be that we suffer with him, that we may be also glorified together. 18 For I reckon that the sufferings of this present time are not worthy to be compared with the glory which shall be revealed in us.* (Emphasis Added).

3. Jesus Teaching Religious Leaders the True Nature of Man -

John 10:

31 Then the Jews took up stones again to stone him. 32 Jesus answered them, Many good works have I shewed you from my Father; for which of those works do ye stone me? 33 **The Jews answered him, saying, For a good work we stone thee not; but for blasphemy; and because that thou, being a man, makest thyself God. 34 Jesus answered them, Is it not written in your law, I said, Ye are gods? 35 If he called them gods, unto whom the word of God came, and the scripture cannot be broken; 36 Say ye of him, whom the Father hath sanctified, and sent into the world, Thou blasphemest; because I said, I am the Son of God?** *37 If I do not the works of my Father, believe me not. 38 But if I do, though ye believe not me, believe the works: that ye may know, and believe, that the Father is in me, and I in him. 39 Therefore they sought again to take him: but he escaped out of their hand, 40 And went away again beyond Jordan into the place where John at first baptized; and there he abode.*

41 And many resorted unto him, and said, John did no miracle: but all things that John spake of this man were true.
42 And many believed on him there. (Emphasis Added)

A few years ago in my capacity as a representative of The Church of Jesus Christ of Latter-day Saints on the Interfaith Counsel of Metropolitan Washington, D.C. (IFC), I was asked by one of the Muslim leaders to speak at his Mosque. As I prayed about how we could find common ground, the thought came that this world is just one big classroom for our Heavenly Father's children. We are all truly brothers and sisters with one Heavenly Father. I decided to share with them Christian teaching about the true nature of man: That we are children of God and joint heirs with our Savior, Jesus Christ. Despite what I had heard about zealous enforcement of blasphemy laws by members of the Muslim faith, my remarks were well received. I believe the Holy Spirit assisted in conveying the message that men and women truly have divine potential.

A lack of understanding of our potential as children of God is much more prevalent than one might expect – even among educated Christians who study the Bible. From time-to-time Sharon and I would invite some of the new friends we met while on our mission in Alabama to the mission home to learn about the Restoration of the Gospel. Members of The Church of Jesus Christ of Latter-day Saints believe that the Lord needed to restore Priesthood authority found in the ancient Church in preparation for the Savior's return to Earth. Those investigating The Church of Jesus Christ of Latter-day Saints are invited to participate in several lessons taught by the missionaries, ask questions, and attend Church services. One family that was very kind to us while we were in Alabama accepted our invitation to be taught the missionary lessons at the mission home and attend Church services with us. We also attended services at their Church – a very large Protestant congregation. While attending Sunday School with us at the local Latter-day Saint Chapel, one of the members of the family asked for a Sunday School manual. Later, after completing the series of lessons at the mission home, I asked the family to be baptized members of The Church of Jesus Christ of Latter-day Saints. The father's answer surprised me. He pulled out the Sunday School manual, which he had by then read from cover to cover, and pointed to the last chapter. The subject of that chapter was "Exaltation". The chapter explained the lesson Paul was teaching the Athenians and the Romans; and the lesson the Savior was teaching the Jewish leaders: The lesson teaches that "We are literally children of the living God." He said: "I could never join your Church. This last chapter is blasphemy."

The mother in the family then supported her husband saying: "We are just worms in comparison with God." She was deeply offended by our doctrine. That ended our effort to teach them about the Restoration of our Lord's Gospel, but I have not forgotten the lesson she taught me. She is correct in her understanding that we are nothing in comparison with God. Moses learned that lesson in his interaction with God. However, she clearly does not understand man's potential to become like God. We are his children and joint heirs with Christ. To reach our potential, we must understand our divine potential; or we will never make the effort to strive to be perfect and become like our Savior and Heavenly Father. As our Lord put the matter as He preached what we call the Sermon on the Mount recorded in Matthew 5:48: - *Be ye therefore perfect, even as your Father which is in heaven is perfect.*

We refer to Jesus Christ as our Savior and Redeemer. Christian doctrine is that our Heavenly Father sent His Only Begotten Son to be sacrificed on the cross at Calvary and atone for the sins of the world. If man will repent of his sins, the Savior's atonement will save him; but man cannot be saved without the Savior's help – no matter how hard he tries. I have often wondered why our Heavenly Father would require the sacrifice of His Son, Jesus Christ, as part of the plan of salvation. After all, He is God, and He has the power to dictate the terms of salvation. Once while giving a talk at the New Albany Mississippi Branch of The Church of Jesus Christ of Latter-day Saints, I shared with those attending my question about why our Heavenly Father would require Jesus to be persecuted and killed on the cross, much less endure the agony of Gethsemane. After the service was over, an elderly man came up to me and shared this thought: The God of Heaven and Father of our Savior Jesus Christ would never require such a sacrifice to save anyone that was not also His child. The Spirit immediately bore witness to me that I had received my answer: God, our Heavenly Father, loves us and sent His Son to draw all His children to Him. God's love is eternal and deep for us. To demonstrate the depth of God's love and give us the strongest possible desire to become like our Savior, the sacrifice of Jesus Christ was necessary. When we really understand the depth of God's love for us and the commitment and sacrifice of our Savior, most of us will want to repent and obey our Heavenly Father's commandments. That is the only way we can become like Him and reach our potential as His heirs. During his mortal ministry the Lord said that His death would draw men to Him -

John 12:

*23 ¶ And Jesus answered them, saying, The hour is come, that the Son of man should be glorified. 24 Verily, verily, I say unto you, Except a corn of wheat fall into the ground and die, it abideth alone: but if it die, it bringeth forth much fruit. 25 He that loveth his life shall lose it; and he that hateth his life in this world shall keep it unto life eternal. 26 If any man serve me, let him follow me; and where I am, there shall also my servant be: if any man serve me, him will my Father honour. 27 Now is my soul troubled; and what shall I say? Father, save me from this hour: but for this cause came I unto this hour. 28 Father, glorify thy name. Then came there a voice from heaven, saying, I have both glorified it, and will glorify it again. 29 The people therefore, that stood by, and heard it, said that it thundered: others said, An angel spake to him. 30 Jesus answered and said, This voice came not because of me, but for your sakes. 31 Now is the judgment of this world: now shall the prince of this world be cast out. 32 **And I, if I be lifted up from the earth, will draw all men unto me.** 33 This he said, signifying what death he should die.*

For thousands of years prophets have written about the times in which we are living. If the God of Heaven, who is our Father, loves us enough to send Jesus Christ to teach us, set an example for us, and then suffer and die to draw us to Him; why would He not give us a sign that we cannot mistake that

He is now preparing to send Jesus once again as prophesied? In the Old Testament Book of Isaiah, we have a very specific prophecy about an event that will occur in the last days before our Lord returns in glory to the Earth. Isaiah was referring to the Book of Mormon, published to the world in our day.

Isaiah 29:

11 And the vision of all is become unto you as the words of a book that is sealed, which men deliver to one that is learned, saying, Read this, I pray thee: and he saith, I cannot; for it is sealed: 12 And the book is delivered to him that is not learned, saying, Read this, I pray thee: and he saith, I am not learned. 13 ¶ Wherefore the Lord said, Forasmuch as this people draw near me with their mouth, and with their lips do honour me, but have removed their heart far from me, and their fear toward me is taught by the precept of men: 14 Therefore, behold, I will proceed to do a marvellous work among this people, even a marvellous work and a wonder: for the wisdom of their wise men shall perish, and the understanding of their prudent men shall be hid.

The "book that is sealed" refers to the Book of Mormon, which the Prophet Joseph Smith was in the process of translating from ancient records that had been buried in the ground for over a thousand years – a part of which was sealed.

Compare what actually happened in our time as recorded by the Prophet Joseph Smith. Martin Harris, a wealthy farmer, had helped Joseph, gave him financial assistance, and was anxious to get confirmation that Joseph's translation of ancient records by revelation was correct. In 1828 Joseph sent Martin to New York City with a copy of ancient characters and some of the translated pages translated from pages in the Book of Mormon. Martin Harris found Professor Charles Anthon, an expert in ancient languages, to confirm the accuracy of the translation. Here is the account of that event as recorded in Joseph Smith - History, a part of Latter-day scripture known as The Pearl of Great Price:

Pearl of Great Price, Joseph Smith - History

61 The excitement, however, still continued, and rumor with her thousand tongues was all the time employed in circulating falsehoods about my father's family, and about myself. If I were to relate a thousandth part of them, it would fill up volumes. The persecution, however, became so intolerable that I was under the necessity of leaving Manchester, and going with my wife to Susquehanna county, in the State of Pennsylvania. While preparing to start—being very poor, and the persecution so heavy upon us that there was no probability that we would ever be otherwise—in the midst of our afflictions we found a friend in a gentleman by the name of Martin Harris, who came to us and gave me fifty dollars to assist us on our journey. Mr. Harris was a resident of Palmyra township, Wayne county, in the State of New York, and a farmer of respectability. 62 By this timely aid was I enabled to reach the place of my destination in Pennsylvania; and immediately after my arrival there I commenced copying the characters off the plates. I copied a considerable number of them, and by means of the Urim and Thummim I translated some of them, which I did between the time I arrived at the house of my wife's father, in the month of December, and the February following. 63 Sometime in this month of February, the aforementioned Mr. Martin Harris came to our place, got the characters which I had drawn off the plates, and started with them to the city of New York. For what took place relative to him and the characters, I refer to his own account of the circumstances, as he related them to me after his return, which was as follows: 64 *"I went to the city of New York, and presented the characters which had been translated, with the translation thereof, to Professor Charles Anthon, a gentleman celebrated for his literary attainments. Professor Anthon stated that the translation was correct, more so than any he had before seen translated from the Egyptian. I then showed him those which were not yet translated, and he said that they were Egyptian, Chaldaic, Assyriac, and Arabic; and he said they were true characters. He gave me a certificate, certifying to the people of Palmyra that they were true characters, and that the translation of such of them as had been translated was also correct. I took the certificate and put it into my pocket, and was just leaving the house, when Mr. Anthon called me back, and asked me how the young man found out that there were gold plates in the place where he found them. I answered that an angel of God had revealed it unto him.* 65 *"He then said to me, 'Let me see that certificate.' I accordingly took it out of my pocket and gave it to him, when he took it and tore it to pieces, saying that there was no such thing now as ministering of angels, and that if I would bring the plates to him he would translate them. I informed him that part of the plates were sealed, and that I was forbidden to bring them. He replied, 'I cannot read a sealed book.' I left him and went to Dr. Mitchell, who sanctioned what Professor Anthon had said respecting both the characters and the translation."*

We should not be surprised that our Heavenly Father would inspire the prophet Isaiah to give such a specific prophecy in view of the marvelous works recorded in the scriptures. However, to me, Isaiah's specific prophecy is astonishing.

That prophecy alone should inspire our Heavenly Father's children to read the Book of Mormon and prepare to receive the Lord upon his return.

In the Alabama Birmingham Mission, we baptized very few preachers of other faiths. However, preachers in the South converting to The Church of Jesus Christ of Latter-day Saints is not unknown. I want to share the story of one preacher's journey to embrace our Lord's Restored Gospel. I will not use his full name here, because he has since passed away and I do not know his family to get their permission. When we met Tony, he had just retired from the ministry as a Baptist preacher. He was in his 60's, had grown up in Atlanta, and knew Martin Luther King from his youth. Tony was African American, and as I got to know him, I learned that he was a powerful preacher of our Lord's Gospel. Before his retirement, Tony had been pastor at some of the largest primarily African American Churches in the South. Here is the story of Tony's conversion as related to me by Tony and the missionaries who taught him.

One of our young missionaries and his companion entered a Post Office and saw a tall black man talking to someone. He heard the man speak about Jesus Christ to the person he was speaking to, and patiently waited until the conversation was over before approaching Tony. He observed that Tony was addressing CD's to be mailed, and later learned that Tony was a singer. Our missionary asked Tony if he would like to know more about Jesus Christ. Tony answered in the affirmative. It is strong evidence of sensitivity to the Spirit and humility that this accomplished preacher, who had been preaching the Gospel his whole life, would humble himself to be instructed by a young missionary.

Not long after the Post Office encounter, the missionaries teaching Tony invited him to a zone conference. In the Alabama Birmingham Mission, we had 5 zones. To make it easier to work with members of the Church, I organized our zones to follow the boundaries of our Stakes. Our Stakes each had about 10 units we call Wards (a small congregation is called a branch if not large enough to be a Ward). Whether a Ward or Branch, each would usually have at least 2 missionaries assigned to it. Members and missionaries attend the unit within the boundaries where they live. Thus, at a zone conference we would have 20 to 30 young missionaries serving within that Stake's boundaries, plus Senior adult full time missionaries that helped in administration. Members of the Stake would assist at each conference to feed lunch to everyone attending. At some point during each zone conference, we would focus on a principle of our Lord's Gospel in a formal program. When it came time for me to address this particular conference, I looked out and saw Tony. He was hard to miss, since at that time we only had one other African American serving in the Alabama Birmingham Mission – a young missionary from Jamaica.

The Gospel topic that I chose for that conference was a passage from the New Testament. The Lord asked his disciples what people were saying about him, and then asked his disciples who they thought he was. Peter said that he was the Christ, the Son of God. The Lord blessed Peter and said that his Father in Heaven revealed that to him. The Lord then told

Peter that he would build his Church upon that rock. Here is the scripture –

Matthew 16:

*13 ¶ When Jesus came into the coasts of Cæsarea Philippi, he asked his disciples, saying, Whom do men say that I the Son of man am? 14 And they said, Some say that thou art John the Baptist: some, Elias; and others, Jeremias, or one of the prophets. 15 **He saith unto them, But whom say ye that I am? 16 And Simon Peter answered and said, Thou art the Christ, the Son of the living God. 17 And Jesus answered and said unto him, Blessed art thou, Simon Bar-jona: for flesh and blood hath not revealed it unto thee, but my Father which is in heaven. 18 And I say also unto thee, That thou art Peter, and upon this rock I will build my church; and the gates of hell shall not prevail against it.** 19 And I will give unto thee the keys of the kingdom of heaven: and whatsoever thou shalt bind on earth shall be bound in heaven: and whatsoever thou shalt loose on earth shall be loosed in heaven. 20 Then charged he his disciples that they should tell no man that he was Jesus the Christ.*

In my message to those attending the conference, I said that the "rock" was not Peter, but was the rock of revelation.

After the conference ended, I had the opportunity to speak briefly with Tony. He told me that he had been arguing with his fellow preachers for most of his life about the meaning of that scripture. Tony was certain that the Lord meant the "Rock of Revelation"; not the "Rock of the man, Peter." Not long after the conference Sharon and I were able to attend Tony's baptism. I am including the story of Tony becoming a member of The Church of Jesus Christ of Latter-day

Saints,because I want to share Tony's way of conveying to others the importance of reading the Book of Mormon.

As far as I am aware, the Book of Mormon is the only book of scripture that has a promise from the Lord given by a prophet that specifically promises revelation to reveal its truth. The promise is found in verses 3-5 of the last chapter in the last division of the Book of Mormon, which is named the Book of Moroni. I am including all of Moroni, Chapter 10, in the Appendix, **NOTE 2** (Page 196). Here are verses 3-5 that I have highlighted:

> *3 Behold, I would exhort you that when ye shall read these things, if it be wisdom in God that ye should read them, that ye would remember how merciful the Lord hath been unto the children of men, from the creation of Adam even down until the time that ye shall receive these things, and ponder it in your hearts. 4 And when ye shall receive these things, I would exhort you that ye would ask God, the Eternal Father, in the name of Christ, if these things are not true; and if ye shall ask with a sincere heart, with real intent, having faith in Christ, he will manifest the truth of it unto you, by the power of the Holy Ghost. 5 And by the power of the Holy Ghost ye may know the truth of all things.*

When you read the Book of Mormon, be careful to follow the instruction given in verse 4, that you read with *sincere heart, with real intent, having faith in Christ.* You don't want to make the mistake that I made. I was first introduced to the Book of Mormon by my supervising editor at the George Washington University Law Review, Cliff Fleming. Cliff is now a Professor of Law at the J. Reuben Clark Law School at Brigham Young University. I read it as an intellectual exercise, not in the way the Lord instructed. When, ten years later, I finally read the Book of Mormon in the way the Lord intended, I knew for certain that the Book of Mormon was the word of God before I finished the first book of Nephi. There the ancient prophet Nephi prophecies the coming forth of the United States as home for liberty upon the earth. First Nephi was written about six hundred years before Christ; and published to the world in 1830. In 1830 the United States was not a significant player on the world stage. The French author, Alexis de Tocqueville, who wrote about the great potential of the United States in his book, *Democracy in America*, didn't publish his feelings about the United States of America until after his travels in the New World in 1831 and 1832.

Tony was in great demand by the missionaries as a speaker. He had a powerful way of getting his message across; and was particularly effective in getting investigators to want to read the Book of Mormon. The Alabama Birmingham Mission had a geographic area that included most of Alabama, a small section of southern Tennessee, and the Northeastern part of Mississippi. I recall that we had a young missionary serving in the extreme Northeast area of Mississippi who was teaching a black Baptist preacher in that area. He asked me if I could get Tony to come preach to that pastor's entire congregation. That request meant that I had to bring Tony up from his then home in Montgomery, where Tony was a great member missionary, and take him several hundred miles to preach in Mississippi. I told the missionary that if he could get the preacher and his congregation to come to our chapel in that area, I would ask Tony to come. Soon, I got word that all was arranged. Sharon and I drove with Tony to Mississippi; and met with the Stake President and Bishop for that Stake and Ward. When we walked into our Chapel, it was filled with members of the black preacher's church. We invited our visiting preacher and the young missionary to speak first, and then came Tony's turn, as guest speaker, to preach to them. I will likely never forget the way Tony got his message across that everyone needed to read the Book of Mormon. The missionaries had done their homework and, acting with faith that Tony would be effective in persuading those attending to read the Book of Mormon, they had enough copies available for each person to have one. When the meeting ended, I learned that every single guest left with a copy of the Book of Mormon.

After Tony told the congregation of how he came to be baptized a member of The Church of Jesus Christ of Latter-day Saints, and the importance of the Book of Mormon in his conversion, he spelled out for them how we often do not give proper priority to things that are really important – the most important being the Word of God. To the best of my memory, here are the words that Tony spoke concerning trust and reading the Book of Mormon:

> *When you get on an airplane, you go back to your seat and sit down. Up in the cockpit are pilots that wear a uniform, but you don't know them. They have stripes on their shoulders, and a nametag identifying them as pilots, but you don't know them. They could be total impostors for all you know. You sit down, don't worry about the people who have your life in their hands, and relax.* ***WHY WON'T YOU READ THE BOOK OF MORMON?***

*When you get sick and go to the drug store to get your prescription filled, you walk up to the pharmacist's counter and give him the paper. The person(s) behind the counter have on white coats, with writing that says "Pharmacist", but you don't know them or anything about them. The person may or may not be a real pharmacist or know anything about medicine – you just don't know. Yet when the person in the white coat gives you those pills, you will take them home and swallow them. **WHY WON'T YOU READ THE BOOK OF MORMON?***

Tony's message to the Mississippi investigators was that the Book of Mormon is the Word of God. It contains messages from our Savior and prophets of the Lord that they have not read; and at a minimum they should read for themselves what the Lord and His prophets have to say to them. Unlike the risk of flying miles above the earth in an airplane controlled by people you don't know; or taking pills of unknown composition given to you by people you don't know; the risk of reading the Book of Mormon is zero; and the potential benefit of reading the Book of Mormon is enormous, with eternal positive consequences.

Finally, Tony shared with his audience the promise in Moroni 10:3-5 at the end of the Book of Mormon. He urged them to test the Lord. Read the Book of Mormon with an honest heart, with sincere intent to learn of its truth, and the Lord would reveal its truth to them by the power of the Holy Spirit if they would just ask Him. Tony said: "When the Spirit reveals a truth to you, you can know for certain that the truth comes from God Himself. Never, never, never let some man take away from you a truth that you have learned from God."

Chapter Two

Evidence – The Three Witnesses

There is power in testimony that the Book of Mormon is the word of God that came from three witnesses who dissented from and left The Church of Jesus Christ of Latter-day Saints after giving that testimony; but continued to confirm the truth of the Book of Mormon until their death.

When Joseph Smith was translating the Book of Mormon, he was specifically instructed by the Lord not to allow anyone else to see the gold plates from which the Book of Mormon was translated. Ten years after first being introduced to The Church of Jesus Christ of Latter-day Saints, and thereafter the Book of Mormon, I seriously read the Book of Mormon as instructed by the prophet, Moroni. As I was preparing to be baptized a member of the Church, I remember asking the missionaries about the location of the golden plates from which the Book of Mormon was translated. At the time I asked the question, my baptism did not depend on their answer, because I had received a witness from the Holy Spirit that the Book of Mormon was the word of God. Rather, I was conscious of the burden the Prophet Joseph Smith must have carried as the only one on the Earth allowed to see the golden plates, then over 1000 years old, upon which words of the Book of Mormon were engraved in an ancient language. I was curious to know the current location of the golden plates.

The missionaries answered that upon completion of his translation of the Book of Mormon, Joseph delivered the gold plates to an angel of God.

Could it be that reliable evidence is available in our time that angels really exist? I learned that while translating the ancient record that we now know as the Book of Mormon, Joseph discovered that there were to be witnesses approved by the Lord to see the Book of Mormon. Joseph was excited to find that he would finally have witnesses to support his testimony that our Heavenly Father, Jesus Christ, and angels were real; and that the golden plates really existed.

The Book of Mormon proves itself to our Heavenly Father's children, whom we are. That proof comes via testimony to our eternal spirits from the Holy Spirit. If we humble ourselves before the Lord, we will know that the doctrine and truths revealed in the Book of Mormon are true because the Spirit of the Lord will testify of truth to us. Nevertheless, our Heavenly Father and our Savior, Jesus Christ, want to make sure that those who are seeking for truth have every opportunity to find truth. The Testimony of the Three Witnesses, found in the beginning of the Book of Mormon, is part of the evidence prepared and presented by God to assist us in our mortal journey.

While serving as a mission president in Alabama, I received a call from one of the General Authorities of The

Church of Jesus Christ of Latter-day Saints. His name was Yoshihiko (Yosh) Kikuchi, and he announced that he would be coming to tour our mission. Elder Kikuchi, who over time became my friend and came to visit us after Sharon and I completed our three-year mission, agreed to speak at two firesides in the Mission – one near Birmingham and one in Huntsville. Elder Kikuchi joined the Church in Japan in his late teens shortly after World War Two. I was very interested in having him share his testimony and his conversion story to our missionaries, members, and to those investigating The Church of Jesus Christ of Latter-day Saints. I did not expect him to ask me to also speak at the firesides – but when he agreed to speak he asked me to join him on the program. I received no specific assignment from Elder Kikuchi, so I prayed about the subject I should address at our two firesides. I knew that we would have investigators attending, several of whom were also lawyers.

I soon felt the strong impression to speak about the three witnesses whose testimony is present at the beginning of every edition of what has now become many, many millions of copies of the Book of Mormon. As a trial lawyer, I am sensitive to the quality of evidence. While preparing my talk for Elder Kikuchi's firesides, I became convinced that the Lord is mindful of the quality of evidence and the effect that evidence will have on us.

Just after the Introduction Page of the Book of Mormon, we find the "Testimony of Three Witnesses." It is placed before the "Testimony of Eight Witnesses" and "Testimony of The Prophet Joseph Smith." I believe the placement of "Testimony of Three Witnesses" is in recognition of the relative value of their testimony as evidence of the truth of the Book of Mormon. All three of the witnesses left The Church of Jesus Christ of Latter-day Saints after adding their written testimony of the truth of the Book of Mormon. Two of the three came back into the Church. David Whitmer never did come back. Even though the three witnesses, Oliver Cowdery, Martin Harris, and David Whitmer, became hostile to the Church and Joseph Smith, not one of them ever denied his testimony of the truth of the Book of Mormon.

Oliver Cowdery earned his living as a schoolteacher, and later in the practice of law. Oliver was one of the scribes that assisted Joseph Smith during the translation of the Book of Mormon and was present when Priesthood authority was first restored by the resurrected John the Baptist. Once when prosecuting a murder case before a jury, after Oliver left the Church, defense counsel tried to cast doubt on the prosecution case because of Oliver's testimony as one of the three witnesses to the Book of Mormon. Oliver replied: *I saw the angel and heard his voice—how can I deny it? It happened in the daytime when the sun was shining bright in the firmament; not in the night when I was asleep. That glorious messenger from heaven, dressed in white, standing above the ground, in a glory I have never seen anything to compare, with the sun insignificant in comparison, and these personages told us if we denied that testimony there is no forgiveness in this life nor in the world to come. Now how can I deny it—I dare not; I will not! (An Address Delivered by Judge C. M. Nielsen in the Twenty-fourth Ward Meeting House, Salt Lake City, Utah, February 20, 1910).* Fellow witness, David Whitmer, in his book published in 1887, made the following statement:

> *I also testify to the world, that neither Oliver Cowdery or*
> *Martin Harris ever at any time denied their testimony.*
> *They both died reaffirming the truth of the divine authen-*
> *ticity of the Book of Mormon. I was present at the death*
> *bed of Oliver Cowdery, and his last words were,"***Brother**
> **David, be true to your testimony to the Book of Mormon."**
> *He died here in Richmond, Mo., on March 3d, 1850. (David*
> *Whitmer, "An Address to All Believers in Christ", page 8).*

Oliver's experience as one of the three witnesses, however, was not his first encounter with beings from the world that we cannot see with our natural eyes. When Oliver Cowdery was acting as scribe for Joseph Smith as Joseph translated the Book of Mormon from the gold plates, a heavenly being came to earth, laid his hands on Oliver's head and ordained him to the Priesthood. If such a meeting with a heavenly being happened to any mortal, they would be excited. Oliver was no exception. Oliver's account as recorded by Joseph Smith who, along with Oliver, was ordained to the Priesthood by the resurrected John the Baptist is included in **NOTE 3** in the Appendix (Page 199). Here are the words that John the Baptist spoke in ordaining Oliver to the Priesthood:

> 'Upon you my fellow-servants, in the name of Messiah, I
> confer this Priesthood and this authority, which shall remain
> upon earth, that the Sons of Levi may yet offer an offering
> unto the Lord in righteousness!'

Martin Harris provided critical financial aid to Joseph Smith at the very beginning of the process of translation of the characters on the golden plates into English of what became the

Book of Mormon. His efforts to find an expert to verify the accuracy of the translation were prophesied by the ancient Prophet Isaiah as recorded in the Old Testament of the Bible. Martin also mortgaged his farm to finance the printing of the first 5000 copies of the Book of Mormon in Palmyra, New York. His support for the Prophet Joseph Smith was opposed by some in his family, and he eventually left the Church. He was chosen by the Lord to be one of the three witnesses to the Book of Mormon; but Martin did not become a witness without some difficulty. Despite Martin's critical contributions to the restoration of our Lord's Gospel, the angel of the Lord would not appear to Martin until he repented and humbled himself before the Lord. When Martin realized that his pride was causing difficulty receiving revelation, he absented himself and prayed for forgiveness. His sincere prayer was accepted; and he was allowed to see and hear the angel as the golden plates from which the Book of Mormon was translated were shown to him. Martin subsequently left the Church, but later in life came back, and at his death was a faithful member. Martin Harris never denied "The Testimony of Three Witnesses" that he signed, despite having had ample opportunity to deny that he had seen an angel and seen and felt with his hands the golden plates upon which the ancient characters were written.

David Whitmer, the third witness who signed "The Testimony of Three Witnesses" introducing the Book of Mormon, also later left The Church of Jesus Christ of Latter-day Saints. He became a prominent citizen in Missouri. Despite his negative feelings about Joseph Smith and The Church of Jesus Christ of Latter-day Saints, David Whitmer was a man of his word. He had been commanded by the voice of the Lord to bear witness of what he saw, heard, and felt concerning the gold plates where the ancient characters were written from which the Book of Mormon was translated.

During the 50 years intervening between his excommunication from The Church of Jesus Christ of Latter-day Saints and his death, David Whitmer never rejoined the Church. During his 50 years outside the Church, many enemies of the Church and others gave David an opportunity to deny his statement as recorded in "The Testimony of Three Witnesses." As recorded in an article entitled "The Last Witness of the Three Witnesses" by Michael R. Morris, published in the January 2020 issue of *The New Era*, a magazine published by The Church of Jesus Christ of Latter-day Saints, David affirmed at the end of this life that he never denied his testimony of the truth of the Book of Mormon:

"A year before his death in Richmond, Missouri, David responded to two encyclopedias that claimed he and the other Witnesses had denied their testimonies of the Book of Mormon.

He declared: *'I will say once more to all mankind, that I have never at any time denied that testimony or any part thereof. I also testify to the world, that neither Oliver Cowdery or Martin Harris ever at any time denied their testimony. They both died affirming the truth of the divine authenticity of the Book of Mormon.'*

Three days before David died, on January 25, 1888, he called his family and his doctor to his bedside. 'Doctor, do you consider that I am in my right mind?' he asked. His doctor replied, 'Yes, you are in your right mind.'

Then David turned to his family and said: '*I want to give you my dying testimony. You must be faithful in Christ. I want to say to you all that the Bible and the record of the Nephites, the Book of Mormon, are true, so you can say that you have heard me bear my testimony on my deathbed.*'"

Here is *The Testimony of Three Witnesses* as recorded in the introductory section of the Book of Mormon:

THE TESTIMONY OF THREE WITNESSES

Be it known unto all nations, kindreds, tongues, and people, unto whom this work shall come: That we, through the grace of God the Father, and our Lord Jesus Christ, have seen the plates which contain this record, which is a record of the people of Nephi, and also of the Lamanites, their brethren, and also of the people of Jared, who came from the tower of which hath been spoken. And we also know that they have been translated by the gift and power of God, for his voice hath declared it unto us; wherefore we know of a surety that the work is true. And we also testify that we have seen the engravings which are upon the plates; and they have been shown unto us by the power of God, and not of man. And we declare with words of soberness, that an angel of God came down from heaven, and he brought and laid before our eyes, that we beheld and saw the plates, and the engravings thereon; and we know that it is by the grace of God the Father, and our Lord Jesus Christ, that we beheld and bear record that these things are true. And it is marvelous in our eyes. Nevertheless, the voice of the Lord commanded us that we should bear record of it; wherefore, to be obedient unto the commandments of God, we bear testimony of these things. And we know that if we are faithful in Christ, we shall rid our garments of the blood of all men, and be found spotless before the judgment-seat of Christ, and shall

dwell with him eternally in the heavens. And the honor be to
the Father, and to the Son, and to the Holy Ghost, which is one
God. Amen.

—*Oliver Cowdery, David Whitmer, Martin Harris*

From *The Testimony of Three Witnesses* we learn that angels really exist and can carry heavy gold plates. We learn that the voice of God can actually speak to regular folks like Oliver Cowdery, Martin Harris, and David Whitmer. We learn that there is a sphere of existence that is real and exists apart from ordinary mortal experience and can be accessed by faith and obedience to the commandments of our Heavenly Father. We learn that our Heavenly Father and Jesus Christ consider the Book of Mormon of sufficient importance in instructing their children here upon the Earth, that Oliver Cowdery, David Whitmer, and Martin Harris were chosen to be witnesses even though they were imperfect sons of God and would later leave the Restored Church. The power of the evidence of the three witnesses to convince our Heavenly Father's children of the truth of the Book of Mormon – which contains the fullness of the Gospel of Jesus Christ and is another witness, along with the Bible, of the divinity of Jesus Christ and His role as our Redeemer and Savior – is in no small part because Oliver Cowdery, Martin Harris, and David Whitmer continued to affirm the truth of the Book of Mormon despite their estrangement from the Church.

After the fireside with Elder Kikuchi, he thanked me for speaking about the Testimony of the Three Witnesses. One of the attorneys, who attended the fireside and was investigating the Church, came up to me and said that he understood the power of testimony that came from someone apparently testifying against their interest. He said that The Testimony of the Three Witnesses inspired him to read the Book of Mormon.

Reading the Book of Mormon will reveal more evidence that the Book of Mormon is the Word of God and provides proof that our Savior will come again. A knowledge of what is recorded and taught in the Book of Mormon will also dramatically increase understanding of the principles taught in the Holy Bible.

The Book of Mormon records a visit of Jesus Christ to America as a resurrected being and gives an account of events leading up to our Lord's visit here two thousand years ago. Events that happened immediately preceding the Lord's visit to America are a type of events that will occur prior to The Second Coming. The most important knowledge to be gained from reading the Book of Mormon, however, will come from reading the lessons taught by the Lord to the Ancient Americans as recorded in Third and Fourth Nephi. The Lord makes it clear that when the time arrives that we are able to have his words to the Ancient Americans, he will soon return to reign upon the Earth in power and great glory.

Chapter Three

The Visit of Jesus Christ to The Americas

Those who witnessed the Savior's visit to America saw heaven open, and angels ascending and descending upon Jesus the Christ. They also heard the words spoken by our Savior that are being fulfilled in our day. If we deny the spiritual side of life, and ignore the Savior's warning to repent, we do so at our peril.

From the Book of Mormon we learn that Jesus Christ visited the Ancient Americans shortly after his resurrection. The Bible records that during his ministry in Palestine, Jesus told his disciples that he had other sheep, not of that fold, that he also had to visit.

John 10:

11 I am the good shepherd: the good shepherd giveth his life for the sheep. 12 But he that is an hireling, and not the shepherd, whose own the sheep are not, seeth the wolf coming, and leaveth the sheep, and fleeth: and the wolf catcheth them, and scattereth the sheep. 13 The hireling fleeth, because he is an hireling, and careth not for the sheep. 14 I am the good shepherd, and know my sheep, and am known of mine. 15 As the Father knoweth me, even so know I the Father: and I lay down my life for the sheep. **16 And other sheep I have, which are not of this fold: them also I must bring, and they shall hear my voice; and there shall be one fold, and one shepherd.** *17 Therefore doth my Father love me, because I lay down my life, that I might take it again. 18 No man taketh it from me, but I lay it down of myself. I have power to lay it down, and I have power to take it again. This commandment have I received of my Father.* (Emphasis Added).

When He appeared to his sheep in America as recorded in the Book of Mormon, Jesus chose twelve disciples, told them to keep His commandments, and shared with them that our Heavenly Father was allowing Him to tell them about Israelites in Jerusalem; but He was not told to tell the people in Jerusalem about the Israelites who had been led away. **NOTE 4** in the Appendix (Page 202) is the scriptural account as recorded in 3 Nephi 15. Here is verse 21 of 3 Nephi 15 where the Lord plainly tells the ancient Americans that they are the sheep He was referring to during His mortal ministry in Palestine:

> *21 And verily I say unto you, that ye are they of whom I said: Other sheep I have which are not of this fold; them also I must bring, and they shall hear my voice; and there shall be one fold, and one shepherd.*

One of many proofs found in the scriptures, these accounts of our Lord's words as recorded in the Bible and in the Book of Mormon concerning his other sheep answer those who falsely contend that the Jesus Christ of the Bible is a different Jesus Christ than the Jesus Christ of the Book of Mormon.

In the New Testament we have an account of our Savior's ministry in the Old World. In the Book of Mormon, we have an account of the visit of our Savior to America and His teachings in the New World. Together the Bible and Book of Mormon provide two witnesses that Jesus is the Christ, the Son of the Living God, and the Savior of the World. The Church of Jesus Christ of Latter-day Saints added the words "Another Testament of Jesus Christ" as a subtitle to the Book of Mormon in 1982, making clear the role played by the Book of Mormon in fulfilling scripture. Truth is established by the testimony of two or three witnesses. Here are scriptures declaring the principle:

Matthew 18:

*15 ⸬ Moreover if thy brother shall trespass against thee, go and tell him his fault between thee and him alone: if he shall hear thee, thou hast gained thy brother. 16 But if he will not hear thee, then take with thee one or two more, **that in the mouth of two or three witnesses every word may be established.***

2ⁿᵈ Corinthians 13

*1 This is the third time I am coming to you. **In the mouth of two or three witnesses shall every word be established.***

Not only is the Book of Mormon a second witness that Jesus is the Christ; it is proof that Jesus is preparing to obey the Father and return. When He was teaching the members of the tribe of Joseph in America shortly after his resurrection, Jesus plainly taught that when the time came that His words to them were published to the world, it would be a sign to them that the work of the Father in gathering Israel had commenced. The Book of Mormon was published in 1830 and recorded the words of the Savior spoken to ancient Americans of the tribe of Joseph who were led here by God in 600 B.C. They were led out of Jerusalem to escape the wickedness there just before its destruction by the Babylonians. Chapter 21 of 3rd Nephi is extraordinary in its revelations and prophecies directly from the Savior Himself; prophecies made 2000 years ago and published almost 200 years ago. Chapter 21, with its headnote, as found today in the Book of Mormon, is included in **NOTE 5** in the Appendix (Page 203).

We cannot read the words of our Savior as recorded in 3rd Nephi, Chapter 21, without realizing that our Heavenly Father's task to restore Israel and prepare for the return of his Son is happening before our very eyes and is very serious business. We ignore the words of our Heavenly Father and His Son, Jesus Christ at our peril. We must repent and obey our Lord's commandments, or we will certainly face the consequences – a lesson learned by those who lived in the days of Noah. Many in the Americas have been established as a free people and numbered with the House of Israel as prophesied by the Savior and published to the world in our time. But if we don't take the warnings spelled out in the Book of Mormon seriously and repent, we can expect that the events described in the Book of Mormon before the Savior's appearance will be a type of what will happen just before the Savior appears in his glory. The wicked will be destroyed. An account of some of the destruction in America recorded in the Book of Mormon just prior to our Lord's visit about 34 A.D. is found in **NOTE 6** in the Appendix (Page 207).

Not only has the Lord established a free people in the Americas as prophesied 2000 years ago, he has also begun to gather Israel. Even 100 years ago, few people thought that Israelites would return to Palestine, much less establish a Jewish state in ancient Israel. But the Lord had not forgotten his ancient prophesy as recorded in the Book of Mormon. Eleven years after publication of the first 5000 copies of the Book of Mormon, the Lord instructed the young Prophet Joseph Smith to send one of the Apostles of newly organized The Church of Jesus Christ of Latter-day Saints to the Holy Land to dedicate the Holy Land to the return of the Jews. Thus it was that on October 24, 1841, despite poverty and hardship, Apostle Orson Hyde climbed the Mount of Olives and offered a prophetic dedicatory prayer – published to the world at the time. His prayer is found in **NOTE 7** in the Appendix (Page 209).

The Lord continues to fulfill his prophecy to the ancient Nephites as recorded in the Book of Mormon; and as noted in Apostle Orson Hyde's dedicatory prayer on the Mount of Olives in our time. Decades after Orson's Hyde's prayer in 1841, the Zionist movement started with an aim to restore Jews to the Holy Land. World conflict hastened the process; and on May 14, 1948, David Ben-Gurion, then leader of the World Zionist Organization, proclaimed the establishment of the State of Israel. It is interesting to note that 138 years after Orson Hyde's prayer, on October 24, 1979, the then President of The Church of Jesus Christ of Latter-day Saints, Spencer

W. Kimball, traveled to the Holy Land to dedicate a five-acre park on the Mount of Olives now named for Apostle of the Lord, Orson Hyde. Today the Orson Hyde Memorial Garden features an amphitheater overlooking the Kidron Valley and the Old City of Jerusalem.

I became interested in Orson Hyde's mission to Israel shortly after I was baptized a member of The Church of Jesus Christ of Latter-day Saints in 1978. I followed closely President Kimball's visit there in 1979 to dedicate the Orson Hyde Memorial Garden – an event hosted by the then Mayor of Jerusalem, Teddy Kollek. Later that year when my neighbor, a judge in a local circuit court and a good friend, told me that he and his wife were going to visit the Holy Land, I asked him to visit the Orson Hyde Memorial Garden. My friend did so, and when he returned gave me pictures of the Garden, including several taken looking up at the Mount of Olives from the Kidron Valley. My neighbor's visit was in the summer, and the pictures clearly show the Orson Hyde Garden as the only green area on the side of the Mount of Olives facing Jerusalem.

In retelling the account of our Lord's visit to America as recorded in the Book of Mormon, I am reminded of the record in the New Testament of Philip's finding Nathanael:

John 1:

43 ¶ The day following Jesus would go forth into Galilee, and findeth Philip, and saith unto him, Follow me.

44 Now Philip was of Bethsaida, the city of Andrew and Peter.

45 Philip findeth Nathanael, and saith unto him, We have found him, of whom Moses in the law, and the prophets, did write, Jesus of Nazareth, the son of Joseph.

46 And Nathanael said unto him, Can there any good thing come out of Nazareth? Philip saith unto him, Come and see.

47 Jesus saw Nathanael coming to him, and saith of him, Behold an Israelite indeed, in whom is no guile!

48 Nathanael saith unto him, Whence knowest thou me? Jesus answered and said unto him, Before that Philip called thee, when thou wast under the fig tree, I saw thee.

49 Nathanael answered and saith unto him, Rabbi, thou art the Son of God; thou art the King of Israel.

50 Jesus answered and said unto him, Because I said unto thee, I saw thee under the fig tree, believest thou? thou shalt see greater things than these.

51 And he saith unto him, Verily, verily, I say unto you, Hereafter ye shall see heaven open, and the angels of God ascending and descending upon the Son of man.

Those who witnessed the Savior's visit to America saw heaven open, and angels ascending and descending upon Jesus the Christ. They also heard the words spoken by our Savior that are being fulfilled in our day. Early readers of the Book of Mormon were not able to see the marvelous technology of our day that allows the Gospel to be preached throughout the world – a necessary precedent to our Savior's return. But they did witness things that our modern science and technology cannot explain – the spiritual dimension of existence that is just as real as the world that we can see, feel, and touch. Those who deny the spiritual side of life, and ignore the Savior's warning to repent, do so at their peril. The Book of Mormon is a voice of warning to us all that we need to repent or suffer the consequences.

Chapter Four

Samuel the Lamanite – Prophecy of the Savior

Prophets were sent to the Americas to inform the people that the Savior of the world was about to be born. One of those prophets was Samuel the Lamanite, a man of color, chosen by the Lord to reveal to the ancient Americans the signs of the Lord's coming.

I have many friends who are of the black race and think, or once thought, that The Church of Jesus Christ of Latter-day Saints did not favor blacks. Because of family history on my Dad's side, I almost did not consent to baptism when the missionaries asked me to be baptized in 1978. However, the Book of Mormon makes clear the Lord's attitude toward our Heavenly Father's children: We are all part of the same eternal family, the Lord loves us all, and we share the same destiny as heirs of God, and joint heirs with Jesus Christ – just as the Apostle Paul taught the ancient Athenians and Romans. Samuel, the Lamanite prophet, was a person of color who lived in ancient America shortly before our Savior was born. The Book of Mormon records part of Samuel's ministry and his important prophesies about the Savior's birth, ministry, and death. It also records the Savior's high regard for Samuel: The Lord insisted that Samuel's words to the Nephites be recorded as scripture – which they had not been prior to our Savior's visit to America after his resurrection.

As I look back on my decades of membership in our Lord's Restored Church, I recognize now that my reluctance to be baptized before blacks were allowed to hold the Priesthood was pride on my part. The Holy Spirit had revealed to me that the Book of Mormon was the word of God. If that were true, then Joseph Smith was a true Prophet of God, and the Church that Joseph founded was the Lord's Restored Church, established in preparation for the Lord's return. The truth of the Restoration will be confirmed by the Holy Spirit, just as the truth of the Book of Mormon will be confirmed by the Spirit. Honesty and humility on our part are almost always required for the Spirit to act, with the exception that the Lord will forgive whom he will forgive and contact us when he chooses to do so.

If we wish the constant companionship of the Holy Spirit and spiritual power, we must repent and obey our Lord's commandments. Several groups of our black brothers and sisters in Africa – before 1978 - were sufficiently humble and submissive to the Spirit, that they read the Book of Mormon, received a spiritual witness of its truth, organized themselves, followed the Gospel as spelled out in the Book of Mormon, and waited for the Lord to act - as He did in 1978 in answer to sincere prayer from many of our Heavenly

Father's children. However, in early June 1978 when I was contemplating baptism to become a member of The Church of Jesus Christ of Latter-day Saints, Priesthood authority for African Americans had not yet been restored. I told the missionaries that I could never join a church that treated my black brothers and sisters differently from other members. The Lord came to my rescue when President Spencer W. Kimball announced on June 9, 1978, that all worthy males would be allowed to hold the Priesthood.

I was raised in Clarkston, Georgia, about 12 miles east of Atlanta. My father was originally from Dahlonega, Georgia, located in the Appalachian Mountains about 65 miles north, northeast of Atlanta. Although I did not know it when I was considering joining The Church of Jesus Christ of Latter-day Saints, my attitude about racial justice came from my Dad's great-grandfather, William Tate. William was a Baptist preacher/farmer in the North Georgia mountains. In the years leading up to the Civil War in the United States, William and many of his fellow preachers were part of the underground railroad facilitating the exodus of black slaves seeking freedom in the Northern States. Not only did he work to free the slaves, William preached that the Union was given to us by Almighty God; and it was a grievous sin to try to destroy it.

In early 1861 after Georgia seceded from the Union, William and other preachers that thought slavery was evil and acted upon their convictions were rounded up and brought to Dahlonega town square where a scaffold had been erected to hang them. William and Sarah Tate had eight children. The oldest was eighteen-year-old Malinda Tate. When Malinda learned what was happening, she saddled her horse and rode as fast as she could to Dahlonega. When she arrived, the preachers were lined up on the scaffold facing a mob waiting to watch the hanging. Malinda jumped off her horse, climbed onto the scaffold with her dad and the other preachers and faced the mob. It is reported that with great courage, force, and majesty she said:

> *If you are wicked enough to hang a woman, go ahead and hang me along with my father and the others. If you hang me, you may get away with hanging these innocent men. But, know this: I have a photographic memory. I will remember every one of you. The Union is going to win this war. When the Union wins, I will see that every single one of you hang.*

After Malinda spoke to them, the mob and its leaders repented of their design to hang the preachers, and instead sent them to a prison camp for the duration of the Civil War. My great great-grandfather survived the war; and his views on the fundamental rights of man were passed down through the generations of his family to me. I only learned about William Tate because my wife, Sharon, heeded an important teaching of our new church, The Church of Jesus Christ of Latter-day Saints, and researched our family history. At the very next Tate family reunion, Sharon presented the result of her research to family members; and like me, the whole family was proud of our ancestor who stood up for right – even if it would mean his death. Everyone was also in awe of Malinda, whose courage and quick action at a young age at the risk of her own life, saved the preachers from the mob.

Not long ago I shared the story of William and Malinda Tate at a meeting of the Interfaith Counsel of Metropolitan

Washington (IFC). A resolution was before the IFC, sponsored by the representative of one of the Protestant churches, holding that all white people were responsible for slavery, and whites must pay reparations. I told the group that I could not support the resolution, because all white people were not responsible for slavery. William and Malinda acted on principle and defied the majority and the mob. Evil exists in the world, but each of us must choose for ourselves whether to participate in, or support evil. Our Heavenly Father holds us responsible for what we do as individuals, not for what is done by our parents, friends, or associates. The IFC Executive Director, who was of the Jewish faith, then recalled that his family in Florida had stood up and fought slavery in the same period. The resolution did not come to a vote.

We are living in the last days before the Second Coming of our Savior in great glory and power. Our Heavenly Father and Jesus Christ are not leaving us in the dark about what is going to happen. If we have ears to hear, and eyes to see, we can be prepared for what is about to take place. It was the same here in the Americas before the Lord's birth and crucifixion. Prophets were sent to inform the people here that the Savior of the world was about to be born. One of those prophets was Samuel the Lamanite, a man of color, chosen by the Lord to reveal to the ancient Americans the signs of the Lord's coming.

The opening scene of the Book of Mormon records the history of Lehi and his family, beginning at Jerusalem where Lehi, a member of the tribe of Joseph, was preaching to the Jews there that they must repent of their wickedness or be destroyed. The Lord warned Lehi and his family to leave

Jerusalem, or they would be killed, and promised to lead Lehi to a choice land. Laman was one of Lehi's older sons, Nephi was younger. By the time Lehi's family arrived in the Americas, Lehi's family had divided into two groups – those who followed our Lord's commandments and listened to the Spirit, and those who did not. Laman was leader of the rebellious group. Nephi was leader of those who wanted to follow our Lord's commandments. The time came that the Lord warned Nephi to lead his followers away from those following Laman. Thus began the story of the wars and interaction between the Lamanites and Nephites as recorded in the Book of Mormon. To assist the Nephites in distinguishing those who opposed Him, the Lord gave Lamanites a skin of color.

Lehi and his family left Jerusalem in about 600 B.C., journeyed through the wilderness, built a ship designed by the Lord, and sailed to the Americas – spending about a year at sea. After the family divided, Lamanites were always more numerous than Nephites. The Lord preserved the Nephites because of their righteousness; and the Nephites became a prosperous people. As time passed the Nephites began to forget their God and ignore his commandments. Meanwhile, as a result of missionary work by faithful Nephites, many Lamanites repented of the evil they had done and followed the Lord. As the time approached for our Lord to be born into the world, Samuel the Lamanite was instructed by the Lord to call the Nephites to repentance and give them a sign they would recognize when the Lord was born. Samuel's prophecies are recorded in three chapters of Helaman in the Book of Mormon. A part of the record of Samuel as recorded in scripture is included in **NOTE 8** in the Appendix (Page 213).

I have included the prophecies of Samuel as recorded in the Book of Mormon to show that Samuel stands shoulder to shoulder with other prophets as a bold prophet of God. Samuel warned the people and told them of things to come without concern for his own safety – trusting in the Lord to use him as the Lord pleased. When our Savior visited the Americas soon after His resurrection, He made clear the high regard He had for Samuel the Lamanite as recorded in the book of 3rd Nephi in the Book of Mormon. I believe the Lord's instructions to include missing parts of Samuel's prophecies in the records is the only instance we have in scripture where the Lord admonished his servants for failing to record an event in scripture. I have included in **NOTE 9** in the Appendix (Page 221) the scripture where the Lord approves prophesies of Isaiah and commands that prophesies of Samuel the Lamanite be added to the record:

In 3rd Nephi Chapter 23 in the Book of Mormon we learn at least two things:

1. The Lord is very careful about the content of textbooks he uses to teach our Heavenly Father's children during our time in mortality.

2. Righteousness is the key for us, regardless of our race or earthly status. Samuel, a Lamanite and man of color, was chosen as the prophet to give the signs in the Americas of our Lord's birth and death.

I believe that there is another lesson in 3rd Nephi Chapter 23. We live in the latter days before the Second coming of our Savior. There are many today who reject the Prophet Joseph Smith and the Book of Mormon and preach that the Jesus

Christ of the Book of Mormon is a different Jesus Christ than the Jesus Christ of the Bible. Here in 3rd Nephi Chapter 23 we have the Lord, preaching in the Americas after his resurrection, speaking of the Isaiah of the Bible and including the American, Samuel the Lamanite, in the same discourse. Samuel the Lamanite was a man of color and a great prophet of God, just as Isaiah was a great prophet. All the prophesies of both prophets have been, and will be, fulfilled. There is one Jesus Christ, and in 3rd Nephi Chapter 23 we have more evidence that the Jesus Christ who preached in the Americas after his resurrection is the same resurrected Jesus Christ that Mary saw at the tomb. He is the same Jesus Christ that showed His Apostle Thomas, the scars in his hands, his feet and his side. He is the same Jesus Christ that came to America after his resurrection and showed the faithful those same scars. The scripture in the Book of Mormon is found in 3rd Nephi 11 and is included in **NOTE 10** in the Appendix (Page 222).

There are very few instances in scripture where we have a record of our Heavenly Father introducing his Son. This is one of them. The Book of Mormon is exactly what it says it is: Another Testament of Jesus Christ. Those who truly love the Lord will feel a desire to read His words that were spoken in the New World, because those words comprise the fullness of our Lord's Gospel and constitute proof that the Second Coming is on the way.

Chapter Five

Latter-Day Proof of the Truth of the Bible

If we have doubts that the Bible is the Word of God, we need to study the Joseph Smith Translation of the Bible, which makes a few corrections and certifies that the Holy Bible is in fact the Word of God.

The Prophet Joseph Smith was commissioned by the Lord to read and correct some translation and transmission errors in the Bible. Joseph's faithfulness to that assignment provides proof in our day that a Prophet of God certified that the Bible is the Word of God. The problem is that many of our Heavenly Father's children living today say "So what?"

We live in a time when organized religion and belief in God are on the decline. Church attendance and prayer are no longer priorities for many of our Heavenly Father's children. One polling organization that tracks religious popular opinion, the Pew Research Center, reported in December 2021 that in the United States, self-identified Christians made up 63%

of the population. In 2011, ten years earlier, that percentage was 75%. These percentages represent real people who no longer identify themselves as Christians. In the past decade the population in the United States increased from 312 million to 333 million – an increase of 21 million people. During that same ten years, in absolute numbers, there were 24.25 million *fewer* Christians despite the 21 million population growth. There is every reason to believe that the downward trend in professing Christians measured by Pew Research will continue, not just in the United States, but also worldwide.

It is true that fewer professing Christians does not necessarily mean that there are fewer people who believe in God and follow his commandments; but it is a good bet that the experience of the people of our time will not be different from the experience of the Nephites, as recorded in the Book of Mormon, who lived in the Americas for a thousand years. The Nephites who abandoned the Church forgot their God, ignored his commandments, became a wicked people, and were all destroyed about 400 A.D. The antidotes are prayer, humility, repentance, and obedience to our Lord's commandments. The consequences of failing to apply the antidotes are suffering, destruction, and the ultimate time when we understand who we really are – children of the living God – who blew our education while in mortality. Those who follow the principle that we should "eat, drink and be merry, for tomorrow we die and that is the end of it" will learn that we never die. This earth is just a big classroom for our Heavenly Father's children, and we are eternal beings sent here by a loving Heavenly Father to learn to follow the Holy Spirit, serve our fellow beings, and become like our Savior. We will not carry our riches, earthly power, or social status with us after our mortal body dies. When we see in perfect clarity the potential that we were sent here to reach, and rejected, while in mortality, our understanding at that point will provide a perfect hell for us.

Experiences I had while serving in the Alabama Birmingham Mission have become increasingly important for me – perhaps because whenever we serve others, our own learning curve is steep. During the time Sharon and I served, the Church called what are titled "Area Seventies." These area seventies supervised and assisted Church leaders and members in a certain geographic area. They generally served for five or six years and were then released. Sharon and I served under the supervision of great Church leaders; and I want to share a little about one of our leaders - an extraordinary Area Seventy who loved the Lord with all of his heart; and later was called as a General Authority Seventy of The Church of Jesus Christ of Latter-day Saints. Devn Cornish was a Harvard trained pediatric specialist who was at the top of his profession. His specialty was the use of advanced procedures to save high risk newborn babies, and he published regularly about the pioneering work he was doing in scientific journals. Not long before we met Devn, Emory University made him an offer he just could not refuse. Devn and his family moved from the West Coast to Atlanta, Georgia. Since the Alabama Birmingham Mission was in Devn's area, he became our supervising Area Seventy.

Elder Cornish would come to Birmingham to hold a correlation meeting with me and the five Stake presidents in the Alabama Birmingham Mission every three months. He would generally come a day early, meet with me, and then accompany missionaries or members doing missionary work in the evening prior to our quarterly meeting. Over time I learned that Devn walked the walk as well as talked the talk. He was not ashamed of our Lord and His Gospel and delighted in sharing his knowledge. Not only did he serve the Lord by making every effort to preach the Gospel; he also took off time to travel to less served areas of the world to provide medical training. Devn and I became friends.

One day, Devn said to me: "President, there is a book I want you to read. It was written by a professor at one of our major universities in the South; and you need to know what the professor is saying about one of the books that members of The Church of Jesus Christ of Latter-day Saints consider scripture – the Bible. It shows why we need both the Holy Bible and living prophets in our day." Although Devn's request that I read the book was unusual, I knew that he would not have asked me to learn what the professor had to say without a good reason. So, I obtained the book and read it.

I am not going to reveal the title of the book or the professor's name, but if the professor reads this, he will know I am writing about him. The professor's book that Elder Cornish wanted me to read concludes that we cannot trust the Bible because we cannot verify that the scriptures were written by their purported authors. In addition, the scriptures have been changed over time by custodians of source materials to suit political ends and are therefore not reliable records of the Word of God.

As a young man the professor grew up loving the Bible and decided to learn all he could about it. He was admitted to one of the most prestigious Bible colleges in the United States and became a star student. He decided to continue his education and learn to read the ancient Biblical texts in original languages. This quest led him to apply to ivy league universities for an advanced degree. His friends at the Bible college warned that if he continued following the path he was on, those giving him his higher degree would take his testimony away. Sure enough, the more he learned, the more his doubts grew. Finally, now an accomplished scholar, the professor wrote a book questioning the Bible. As polling shows, many are following the same path as the professor; and his book is one of many that is giving an increasing number of our Heavenly Father's children cover to live as they please – ignoring the Lord's commandments when it suits. The Bible is rejected as instruction from the Lord on how we should live our lives; or simply ignored as people decide that each of us, in this classroom we call Earth, should follow a curriculum that we create for ourselves. The Apostle Paul described the condition of the professor and those of similar persuasion in verses 1-9 in his 2ⁿᵈ letter to Timothy in the New Testament:

2ⁿᵈ Timothy CHAPTER 3

1 This know also, that in the last days perilous times shall come.

2 For men shall be lovers of their own selves, covetous, boasters, proud, blasphemers, disobedient to parents, unthankful, unholy,

3 Without natural affection, trucebreakers, false accusers, incontinent, fierce, despisers of those that are good,

4 Traitors, heady, highminded, lovers of pleasures more than lovers of God;

5 Having a form of godliness, but denying the power thereof: from such turn away.

6 For of this sort are they which creep into houses, and lead captive silly women laden with sins, led away with divers lusts,

7 Ever learning, and never able to come to the knowledge of the truth.

*8 Now as Jannes and Jambres withstood Moses, **so do these also resist the truth:** men of corrupt minds, reprobate concerning the faith.*

9 But they shall proceed no further: for their folly shall be manifest unto all men, as theirs also was.

After I read the professor's book, my heart ached for him. If he would believe that God lives, that Jesus is the Christ, and still lives, and that continuing revelation is possible, he could learn for himself that the Bible is the word of God, notwithstanding some potential scribal errors. Our Heavenly Father has not left us without tools to separate truth from error. As in ancient times, we have been given living prophets to guide us.

Ten years ago, I was asked, along with clergy of other faiths, to speak at an interfaith event held in a Sikh temple in Chantilly, Virginia. The event was to show solidarity with victims of a mass shooting on August 5, 2012, in a Sikh temple in Oak Creek, Wisconsin. The last speaker was a Hindu priest. I will not soon forget what he said: "We have had prophets on the earth for thousands of years. It is time we start listening to them."

The prophet our Heavenly Father first called to guide us in our day was the Prophet Joseph Smith. During Joseph's ministry, the Lord gave him the assignment to read the Bible and make necessary corrections. The result of that effort is what is now called the Joseph Smith Translation of the Bible. Short corrections to the text are in footnotes to the King James Version of the Bible published by The Church of Jesus Christ of Latter-day Saints. Longer corrections are published in a separate section labeled: *Joseph Smith Translation Appendix* found at https://www.churchofjesuschrist.org/ , Libraries>Scriptures>Study Helps>Joseph Smith Translation Appendix. In my Quad, the Joseph Smith Translation Appendix is located after the Bible and before the Book of Mormon. After studying the Joseph Smith Translation of the Bible, the conclusion is inescapable that the Lord instructed his Prophet in our time to certify the Bible as the Word of God, because Joseph made very few changes or additions. I expect the professor knows about Joseph's work with the Bible. Perhaps he doesn't believe our Heavenly Father will call a prophet in our time; or perhaps he has reached the point where he doesn't believe he has a Heavenly Father, and when he dies, that is the end of it all.

If the professor, and the increasing number of people who are following in the professor's footsteps, will read the Book of Mormon, pray about it as Moroni directs with an honest heart and real intent in the name of Jesus Christ, the Lord will reveal its truth to them by the power of the Holy Ghost. The reasoning is that if we have revelation from Heaven that the Book of Mormon is the Word of God, then the prophet that gave us the Book of Mormon is a true prophet. If that prophet then certifies the Bible as the Word of God, we have two works of scripture -the Book of Mormon and the Bible - testifying to us that Jesus is the Christ, and that we need to repent and obey the commandments of God to learn the lessons of mortality and reach our divine potential.

Finding that there are very few changes made to the Bible by the Prophet Joseph Smith does not mean that the changes he made are not important. Two of the corrections/additions that are important to me are: First, the change to the Lord's prayer. When preaching what is known as the Sermon on the Mount, the Lord taught his followers how to pray, and gave what we call the "Lord's Prayer" as an example prayer. As a child I learned this prayer, as found in Matthew 6, by heart. The words, "Lead us not into temptation" always bothered me, because I could not imagine our Heavenly Father leading us into temptation. The Prophet Joseph's change to the Lord's prayer is found in footnote a. to verse 13 in Matthew, Chapter 6 of the Joseph Smith Translation of the Bible. The prayer is changed to read: "... and suffer us not to be led into temptation." The Savior was teaching us to ask our Heavenly Father to protect us from being led into temptation – not to implore him not to lead us to do evil.

The second change is an addition to Matthew 9 that records our Lord explaining to Jewish leaders why their baptism is not to be accepted; and in the process identifying Jesus Christ as the God of the Old Testament:

Joseph Smith Translation, Matthew 9:18–21.

Compare Matthew 9:16–17 Jesus rejects the baptism of the Pharisees; it has no value because they do not accept Him. He proclaims that He is the one who gave the law of Moses.

18 Then said the Pharisees unto him, Why will ye not receive us with our baptism, seeing we keep the whole law?

19 But Jesus said unto them, Ye keep not the law. If ye had kept the law, ye would have received me, for I am he who gave the law.

20 I receive not you with your baptism, because it profiteth you nothing.

21 For when that which is new is come, the old is ready to be put away.

In this scripture Jesus proclaims himself the law giver of the Old Testament. He is identifying himself as Jehovah. Without help from the Spirit, which help comes from humility, repentance, and obedience, it is no wonder that the Jews caused the execution of our Lord for blasphemy.

The professor was halted in his progression because he could not get back to original manuscripts that reveal the word of God; and he believes the scripture we now have is corrupted. Perhaps it never occurred to the professor, and those who follow his reasoning, that our Heavenly Father is aware of what is going on in His classroom we call Earth. If God loves His children, would He allow us to attend class with no study guides or lessons? Would He not want teachers for His children? Would He allow Satan to destroy the plan of salvation by depriving us of needed classroom lesson material? The answer to these questions for those of us living in the current age is the same as it was for His children anciently – prophets are called and trained by God to teach us. In fact, once we have a true testimony of Jesus Christ and the Holy Ghost resides in us, we have the Spirit of Prophecy and the ability and duty to teach our brothers and sisters living around us. Here is the scripture in the New Testament:

Revelation 19:

9 And he saith unto me, Write, Blessed are they which are called unto the marriage supper of the Lamb. And he saith unto me, These are the true sayings of God.

*10 And I fell at his feet to worship him. And he said unto me, See thou do it not: I am thy fellowservant, and of thy brethren that have the testimony of Jesus: worship God: **for the testimony of Jesus is the spirit of prophecy.*** (Emphasis added).

Our duty while we are in mortality is to obtain a testimony of Jesus. We do that by humbling ourselves as a little child, asking our Heavenly Father in the name of Jesus Christ to answer our prayer, and then acting upon the revelation that we receive. As the Lord explained in the Sermon on the Mount:

Matthew 7:7

⁊ Ask, and it shall be given you; seek, and ye shall find; knock, and it shall be opened unto you:

8 For every one that asketh receiveth; and he that seeketh findeth; and to him that knocketh it shall be opened.

9 Or what man is there of you, whom if his son ask bread, will he give him a stone?

10 Or if he ask a fish, will he give him a serpent?

11 If ye then, being evil, know how to give good gifts unto your children, how much more shall your Father which is in heaven give good things to them that ask him?

The professor has made the same mistake made by leaders of old. He has looked beyond the mark. In the Book of Mormon we find scripture written by the Prophet Jacob about 550 B.C. prophesying that the Jews would reject our Lord when he came to Earth in mortality to teach them. Jacob 4:10-16 is set forth in **NOTE 11** in the Appendix (Page 225). Verse 14 is a follows:

> *14 But behold, the Jews were a stiffnecked people; and they despised the words of plainness, and killed the prophets, and sought for things that they could not understand. Wherefore, because of their blindness, which blindness came by looking beyond the mark, they must needs fall; for God hath taken away his plainness from them, and delivered unto them many things which they cannot understand, because they desired it. And because they desired it God hath done it, that they may stumble.*

The "mark" referred to in verse 14 is Jesus Christ. This prophecy was given some 500 years before Jesus was born of Mary in Bethlehem. The Lord was inspiring his prophet in the Americas to teach his children the principles of righteousness, and the necessity of looking to our teacher, Jesus Christ, to guide us. If we trust in the Lord, pray to our Heavenly Father in sincere and humble prayer, and obey His commandments, nothing will be able to shake our testimony of Jesus Christ, who is our "mark." The trouble is, if we are not very careful, we will become wise in our own eyes; and like the professor, will deny the faith, look beyond the mark, and kick against the pricks.

The Lord will prevail on the Earth, and no unhallowed hand will be able to stop the advance of the Kingdom of God in preparation for the Second Coming. Times looked very bad just after the Savior's mortal ministry. The Apostle Paul was a prisoner but spoke with boldness to his captors, sharing with them his experience while going to Damascus to persecute followers of Jesus. Undoubtedly Paul thought the Savior was dead, as did almost everyone after His crucifixion. But by the time of his appearance and account before King Agrippa, Paul knew that Jesus Christ still lived and that our Savior was aware of what was happening in the classroom of Earth. I am sure that Paul was astonished that our Lord would choose him to preach the Gospel in view of Paul's previous actions; but the Lord wants us to be either hot or cold, not lukewarm:

Revelation Chapter 3:

15 I know thy works, that thou art neither cold nor hot: I would thou wert cold or hot.

16 So then because thou art lukewarm, and neither cold nor hot, I will spue thee out of my mouth.

17 Because thou sayest, I am rich, and increased with goods, and have need of nothing; and knowest not that thou art wretched, and miserable, and poor, and blind, and naked:

18 I counsel thee to buy of me gold tried in the fire, that thou mayest be rich; and white raiment, that thou mayest be clothed, and that the shame of thy nakedness do not appear; and anoint thine eyes with eyesalve, that thou mayest see.

19 As many as I love, I rebuke and chasten: be zealous therefore, and repent. (Emphasis added).

20 Behold, I stand at the door, and knock: if any man hear my voice, and open the door, I will come in to him, and will sup with him, and he with me.

21 To him that overcometh will I grant to sit with me in my throne, even as I also overcame, and am set down with my Father in his throne.

22 He that hath an ear, let him hear what the Spirit saith unto the churches.

Here are the words that Paul spoke to King Agrippa while he was a prisoner:

Acts 26:

8 Why should it be thought a thing incredible with you, that God should raise the dead?

9 I verily thought with myself, that I ought to do many things contrary to the name of Jesus of Nazareth.

10 Which thing I also did in Jerusalem: and many of the saints did I shut up in prison, having received authority from the chief priests; and when they were put to death, I gave my voice against them.

11 And I punished them oft in every synagogue, and compelled them to blaspheme; and being exceedingly mad against them, I persecuted them even unto strange cities.

12 Whereupon as I went to Damascus with authority and commission from the chief priests,

13 At midday, O king, I saw in the way a light from heaven, above the brightness of the sun, shining round about me and them which journeyed with me.

14 And when we were all fallen to the earth, I heard a voice speaking unto me, and saying in the Hebrew tongue, Saul,

Saul, why persecutest thou me? it is hard for thee to kick against the pricks.

15 And I said, Who art thou, Lord? And he said, I am Jesus whom thou persecutest.

16 But rise, and stand upon thy feet: for I have appeared unto thee for this purpose, to make thee a minister and a witness both of these things which thou hast seen, and of those things in the which I will appear unto thee;

17 Delivering thee from the people, and from the Gentiles, unto whom now I send thee,

18 To open their eyes, and to turn them from darkness to light, and from the power of Satan unto God, that they may receive forgiveness of sins, and inheritance among them which are sanctified by faith that is in me.

The Lord has not put a time limit on learning while we are in mortality. Paul was guilty of gross sins against the Kingdom of God, including that of inciting murder. Yet our Lord called Paul to serve because Paul was needed, was not lukewarm, and was willing to repent and make total commitment to our Lord's cause of teaching our Heavenly Father's children.

We have the choice of becoming like Paul. If we have been cold to the mortal lessons we need to learn, we have the option of becoming hot. If we think we are rich and in need of nothing and are thus unable to see our poverty and nakedness as to eternal things, we have the option to seek and obtain eternal wealth and raiment. The truth is that everything we see with mortal eyes will pass away, including our gold, silver, fine homes, and luxury cars. It is the things we cannot see that will last – things of the spirit. We were alive before the world was created and will be alive after the world ends. We don't want to be like Esau and sell our birthright as an heir of God and joint heir with Jesus Christ for a bowl of soup. If we have doubts that the Bible is the Word of God, we need to study the Joseph Smith Translation of the Bible, which makes a few corrections and certifies that the Holy Bible is in fact the Word of God. After study, if we will pray in humility to know of the truth of the Bible, spiritual confirmation of its truth will come to us from God himself.

Chapter Six

Agency – Essential to the Divine Plan of Salvation

What is in our hearts and minds belongs to us - we have the agency to decide what to think. Those who exercise power over our mortal bodies cannot dictate to us our thoughts and the feelings of our hearts. Our spirits never die, and the choices we make determine our eternal destiny.

In view of man's history of abusing and enslaving his fellow human beings over millennia, those who question that God lives and that we are in fact his children will likely dispute that God requires liberty be an essential part of our mortal experience. Yet the agency of man is something that our Heavenly Father has insisted upon since before man was introduced to the Earth. The problem is that some of our Heavenly Father's children – our brothers and sisters – rebelled; and have continued to rebel since the beginning. The scriptures describe a great war in Heaven at the time of the creation. One of the children of God, Lucifer, wanted to take charge of our mortal education. He told our Father that he, Lucifer, would guarantee that everyone would return home after mortality. To make that guarantee, Lucifer needed to take away the agency, or liberty, of man. Under Lucifer, we would no longer have the right to choose to follow our Heavenly Father's commandments. We would be forced to obey and would therefore never sin or violate the laws of God. In other words, from the beginning, the conflict has been between choosing security or choosing agency. When the choice was put to us and our brothers and sisters before the world was – for we were alive then and have had a veil placed over our memory of premortal life – one third of the hosts of Heaven chose security. That choice meant those choosing security over agency chose to follow Lucifer, or Satan.

Our Heavenly Father had chosen Jesus Christ to manage the education of His children. We have an account of the great value placed on liberty as explained to Moses by our Father in Heaven just after Moses was tempted by Satan. This account is in The Pearl of Great Price, Moses Chapter 4. In my Quad it is located after the Doctrine and Covenants. The Pearl of Great Price can be found on-line at https://www.churchofjesuschrist.org/.

Pearl of Great Price, Moses Chapter 4:

1 And I, the Lord God, spake unto Moses, saying: That Satan, whom thou hast commanded in the name of mine Only Begotten, is the same which was from the beginning, and he came before me, saying—Behold, here am I, send me, I will be thy son, and I will redeem all mankind, that one soul shall not be lost, and surely I will do it; wherefore give me thine honor.

2 But, behold, my Beloved Son, which was my Beloved and Chosen from the beginning, said unto me—Father, thy will be done, and the glory be thine forever.

3 Wherefore, because that Satan rebelled against me, and sought to destroy the agency of man, which I, the Lord God, had given him, and also, that I should give unto him mine own power; by the power of mine Only Begotten, I caused that he should be cast down;

4 And he became Satan, yea, even the devil, the father of all lies, to deceive and to blind men, and to lead them captive at his will, even as many as would not hearken unto my voice.

Our Heavenly Father gave us agency, and he would not let Satan take it away because that would have frustrated the plan of salvation and stopped our progress.

As we look at the world in our time, and as we learn about the experience of those who have gone before us, we realize that many have agency but do not have liberty now, and many did not have liberty in past ages. How is it just for our Heavenly Father to tolerate such disparity in mortal opportunity depending on date and place of birth, and earthly parentage? In ages past, political leaders have dictated every part of mortal life, including mandating the religion of each citizen. In our time, communism declared there was no God, and people of faith have been persecuted and killed. Slavery still exists in parts of the world, and human beings are treated as property. Modern technology makes it possible for oppressors to make merchandise of human hearts and other organs. Scriptures describe the wickedness of man in ages past. We see with our own eyes evil in our time. In some countries faith is dictated by the state, and people think they serve God when they destroy others of differing faiths. Some people deny the existence of God because they reason that no just God would tolerate such wickedness. But behind all conjecture lies eternal truth: This planet is a classroom for our Heavenly Father's children. We are eternal beings and did not begin on Earth; and the end of our mortal experience will not close out our lives. If we live the very best we can while in class on the Earth, our Father in Heaven will make sure that the rest of our education is taken care of.

The Book of Mormon records the experience of two prophets sent to preach the Gospel in a city where the people had become very wicked. As these prophets observed the rulers of the city destroy the followers of Christ by fire and burn their scriptures, they wondered how God could tolerate such an awful scene of wickedness. The scripture is found in Alma, Chapter 14, which is included in **NOTE 12** in the Appendix (Page 226).

It is hard to imagine a more compelling scene: Families with women and children being burned alive. Yet, to preserve agency and give the wicked rulers an opportunity to choose to reject their God, the Prophet Alma – who could have saved his followers by calling down power from Heaven – was prevented by God from saving them. Here is a graphic example of the eternal nature of man, and our accountability before God for what we do. On judgement day the wicked must account for the choices they make in mortality. Agency is vital for eternal progression and is a divine gift to all people. Without agency, we would not be able to gain the knowledge and understanding necessary to reach our potential as sons and daughters of the living God.

Sometimes, however, God does not wait for final judgment day to punish perpetrators of evil. Leaders of the city of Ammonihah, where believing women and children were destroyed by fire and their scriptures burned, were killed while abusing the Prophets Alma and Amulek. An earthquake destroyed the prison, killed the leaders, and freed Alma and Amulek. A few years later, the entire city was destroyed by the Lamanites. The scriptural account from the Book of Mormon is found in Alma 14, verses 23-29; and Alma 25, verse 2, reproduced in **NOTE 13** in the Appendix (Page 228).

The people of Ammonihah were warned by the Prophets Alma and Amulek, sent from God, to repent or be destroyed. Instead of repenting, their leaders ordered that believers in the city be killed. Ammonihah's leaders imprisoned and tortured Alma and Amulek. It was undoubtedly their intent to kill the Prophets after they finished abusing and having fun with them. The Lord destroyed the wicked leaders and people of Ammonihah – all of them – who refused to listen to His Prophets.

We have the agency to follow the example of the leaders and people of Ammonihah and choose evil. However, if we refuse to repent, as did the people of Ammonihah, we do not get to choose the consequences that will flow from our choice. These are the last days before the Second Coming of our Lord. Prophets are calling for us to repent prior to His coming. Events recorded in the Book of Mormon are a type of what will happen on Earth prior to our Lord's return. We would be wise to repent while we can.

Our divine gift of agency can bring freedom of conscience. We can be imprisoned, and our mortal body destroyed by our fellow human beings, but they cannot destroy our spirit or our thought. We are eternal beings. During his mortal ministry, our Lord explained the reality that we often fail to recognize as he instructed his Apostles prior to sending them out to preach:

Matthew 10:

28 And fear not them which kill the body, but are not able to kill the soul: but rather fear him which is able to destroy both soul and body in hell.

What is in our hearts and minds belongs to us - we have the agency to decide what to think. Those who exercise power over our mortal bodies cannot dictate to us our thoughts and the feelings of our hearts. In the Book of Mormon we have an account of a group of Nephites who were enslaved. Even though their oppressors made their lives very difficult, as they repented of their sins, God caused their burdens to be made light and gave them strength. Eventually, after much suffering, they were led to freedom. The scriptural account in the Book of Mormon is found in Mosiah 24, reproduced in **NOTE 14** in the Appendix (Page 229).

Unlike the people of Ammonihah, the people of Alma listened to the teachings of the Prophet Abinadi and repented of their sins. Even though they suffered for their sins, the Lord delivered them.

In modern times we have seen the eternal conflict between security and agency take various forms. Many have lived their lives in slavery and fear. Many have died on one side or the other of this eternal conflict. But one thing is certain: The Gospel of Jesus Christ will go forth upon the Earth, and nothing will stop fulfillment of the ancient and modern prophecies. All will have the opportunity to hear the Word of God; and make a personal decision whether to embrace the Gospel. Anyone with eyes to see and a brain to think in our time can see that the World is changing at an exponential rate. Revelation is being poured out upon man from Heaven and marvelous things are happening. In my Dad's and my lifetimes we have seen amazing changes that have affected the lives of not just the rich and privileged, but also regular folks. Now literally billions of people can hear and see the word of the Lord preached at the same instant. Truth can and does confront error in real time.

The question before each of us is: Will we choose agency and pay the price of agency, or will we choose security – which may seem the correct and sensible choice. History has provided many examples of how to choose: Follow the commandments of God and the choice will be obvious and easy. Ignore the commandments and our choice will lead to slavery and death. Those who decide to advance Lucifer's cause to destroy the agency of man cannot prevail; because all who live on the Earth are of one blood, as stated by the Apostle Paul to the Athenians. We are children of the living God. Our Heavenly Father's children are not slaves.

Chapter Seven

Fear – Enemy of the Plan of Salvation

Using our intelligence before we act will help us to obey God's commandments. Obeying God's commandments will bring the Spirit. The Spirit will bring us knowledge. Knowledge will bring us power. With power, we can overcome fear.

Ever since I began a serious study of the Bible as a young man, I have wondered why the Lord counts the fearful as grievous sinners – to be sent along with murderers, whoremongers, and liars to hell. We all fear at some point, so does the scripture mean that all of God's children will be sent to hell? The scripture I am referring to is found in the next to last chapter of the Book of Revelations in the New Testament of the Bible:

Revelations 21:

7 He that overcometh shall inherit all things; and I will be his God, and he shall be my son.

> 8 But the **fearful**, and unbelieving, and the abominable, and murderers, and whoremongers, and sorcerers, and idolaters, and all liars, shall have their part in the lake which burneth with fire and brimstone: which is the second death. (Emphasis added).

Not only are the fearful included with murderers, whoremongers, sorcerers, idolaters, and liars; but the fearful are at the head of the list. If Satan can get us to fear, then he can control us and get us to do his bidding during our time on earth. There is no dodging the truth – if we want to reach our eternal destiny as children of the Living God, we must learn to overcome fear. We begin the process of overcoming fear by obeying our Lord's commandments. When we obey, the Spirit will come to us. With the Spirit will come real power. Throughout history the Lord as our school master during mortality has had difficulty getting us to complete step one – learning to be obedient.

In the Old Testament of the Bible, we have an account of the Lord revealing his intent to destroy Jerusalem to Jeremiah the Prophet. Jeremiah was told that the people and their leaders were following other Gods, sacrificing their children as burnt offerings to Baal, and filling Jerusalem with the blood of innocents. It was the Lord's intention to kill many and cause inhabitants of the city to suffer famine and become cannibals of their own children. But the Lord offered the people a chance to repent before fulfillment of the prophecy. At that time, around 600 B.C., the people were undoubtedly disobeying all ten commandments given to Moses, but the Lord only demanded obedience to one of them. Here is the scripture:

Jeremiah Chapter 17:

19 ⁊ Thus said the Lord unto me; Go and stand in the gate of the children of the people, whereby the kings of Judah come in, and by the which they go out, and in all the gates of Jerusalem;

20 And say unto them, Hear ye the word of the Lord, ye kings of Judah, and all Judah, and all the inhabitants of Jerusalem, that enter in by these gates:

21 Thus saith the Lord; Take heed to yourselves, and bear no burden on the sabbath day, nor bring it in by the gates of Jerusalem;

22 Neither carry forth a burden out of your houses on the sabbath day, neither do ye any work, but hallow ye the sabbath day, as I commanded your fathers.

23 But they obeyed not, neither inclined their ear, but made their neck stiff, that they might not hear, nor receive instruction.

24 And it shall come to pass, if ye diligently hearken unto me, saith the Lord, to bring in no burden through the gates of this city on the sabbath day, but hallow the sabbath day, to do no work therein;

25 Then shall there enter into the gates of this city kings and princes sitting upon the throne of David, riding in chariots and on horses, they, and their princes, the men of Judah, and the inhabitants of Jerusalem: and this city shall remain for ever.

26 And they shall come from the cities of Judah, and from the places about Jerusalem, and from the land of Benjamin, and from the plain, and from the mountains, and from the south, bringing burnt offerings, and sacrifices, and meat offerings, and incense, and bringing sacrifices of praise, unto the house of the Lord.

27 But if ye will not hearken unto me to hallow the sabbath day, and not to bear a burden, even entering in at the gates of Jerusalem on the sabbath day; then will I kindle a fire in the gates thereof, and it shall devour the palaces of Jerusalem, and it shall not be quenched.

I have often wondered why the Lord made such a sweeping promise of deliverance based upon honoring the Sabbath, as opposed to stopping murder, adultery, theft, and idolatry. I cannot find an explanation in the scriptures, except possibly that the Lord had already tried to get them to obey the other commandments. I believe that the Lord hoped that honoring the Sabbath and keeping it holy would soon lead the people to repent, as they took time to contemplate their sinful conduct. We know that the people did not listen to the words of the Lord as brought to them by the Prophet Jeremiah. They failed to keep the Sabbath Day holy. In 587/586 B.C. Jeremiah's prophesies became reality as the Babylonians brought siege to Jerusalem and captured it.

It has been a consistent practice of our Heavenly Father's children to come to Earth, forget God, make up our own rules, and ignore the rules given to us by God. We become so caught up in the things of the world that we ignore the Holy Spirit. As a result of ignoring the Spirit, we fail to learn who we really are and why we are on Earth in the first place. We become short sighted and live our lives by reacting only to what is right in front of us. We live by giving in to greed, ambition, lust, and fear. We ignore the needs of our fellow human beings; we live to get rich or obtain power; we ignore the law of chastity so we can satisfy lust; and we make decisions based on fear rather than intelligence.

We cannot let our lives be governed by emotion if we want to learn to be perfect like our Savior and our Heavenly Father. There are many examples of wicked human behavior caused by what comes down to a lack of intelligence. An example of such behavior was in the news not very long ago that really struck me. When I heard the report, my immediate reaction was anger and a desire for swift punishment of the person who committed the crime. However, the account of what had happened would not leave me; and I searched for a deeper meaning and lesson from the news report.

A young woman was trying out to be a cheer leader for the football team in her high school. All positions were filled, except for one slot, and the young lady had serious competition for that slot from one of her classmates. If selected, the young woman would only be a cheer leader for a year because she would graduate before the next season. According to the news account, the young woman's mother was very concerned that her daughter's classmate would beat her at the tryouts and get the cheerleading slot; so, the young woman's mother killed her daughter's classmate to eliminate the competition.

The more I thought about this case, the more I knew there was something here for me to learn. The facts were simple enough: Fear of loss and ambition without restraint led to murder. But why would someone commit murder to achieve such a fleeting objective – after all, the cheer leading position would only last for one school year. The more I pondered the news report and the lesson it taught, the more I realized that while very few will go to the extreme taken by the would-be cheerleader's mother, almost all of us are guilty of making important decisions and acting on those decisions without using our God given intelligence and agency to choose the right path.

How about our decision to stop and get that big chocolate shake when we see the sign or hear the advertisement – when we know that our blood glucose level is already through the roof. Or, how about spending the extra money to get that new luxury car when money is already tight, and a much simpler and cheaper car will suffice. How about giving into temptation to view pornography; commit adultery; or have one drink for the road as we leave the bar. How about cheating so that we can pass the test or complete an assignment without studying or making the effort to complete the homework. If we will think about our decisions in life before we act, as God would do, we will be saved from a lot of suffering and heart ache during our mortal journey.

I will never forget an incident during my first year studying chemical engineering at Georgia Tech. A very talented, sharp young man that went to high school with me was in my chemistry class. It was a large class with no proctors for tests, and Johnny thought he could write the formulas on the inside cuffs of his sleeves - and no one could catch him. The professor, however, was sharper than Johnny thought, and his cheating ended his college career. Examples of shortsighted destructive behavior are seen by all of us if we will just open our eyes to see and our ears to hear. The mother in the news report had a perspective of less than a year – the football season. Decisions to engage in gluttony, adultery, and other sins are often made with a time perspective that is near instantaneous. If we have no eternal compass, we cannot reach an eternal destination.

If we will pay attention as we go through life, we will learn from our own experience how to let intelligence govern our lives – as God would have us do. We cannot become perfect in any other way. The Prophet Joseph Smith received a revelation from the Lord that included specific information about how the Lord views intelligence. I had read the scripture, found in the Doctrine and Covenants of the scriptures of The Church of Jesus Christ of Latter-day Saints many times. However, I did not understand its significance until an older, retired member of our Church, who was helping one of our young men repent from serious sin, taught me a lesson. Here is the scripture:

Doctrine and Covenants Section 93:

36 The glory of God is intelligence, or, in other words, light and truth.

This member called me late one night to discuss the young man's progress and asked me if I knew what the scripture meant. I had gone to bed early that night because I was getting up very early the next morning. I was dead asleep when the phone rang and was aggravated at the old man for calling so late. I answered him that I was not sure what he meant, but I was sure that I was about to find out. He could not have missed my sarcastic tone. Undeterred, he delivered his message, which has served me well ever since. Here is what the old man said: "When we use reason and intelligence to govern the actions we take, we are acting like God would act. When we let our behavior be governed by emotion, lust, anger, greed and ambition, or fear, we are acting the opposite of the way God would act."

When life is viewed from a perspective of our mortal journey, which is a small, but very important part of an eternal journey, we can better understand what we need to do as we go through life. Using our intelligence before we act will help us to obey God's commandments. Obeying God's commandments will bring the Spirit. The Spirit will bring us knowledge. Knowledge will bring us power. With power, we can overcome fear.

The Church of Jesus Christ of Latter-day Saints has two very simple sacrament prayers that illustrate the relationship between obeying our Lord's commandments and having the Spirit of the Lord with us as we go through mortality. Here are the prayers as given in the Book of Mormon for the bread and water (Since the early days of the Restored Church in our day, water has been substituted for wine):

Book of Mormon, Moroni Chapter 4:

How elders and priests administer the sacramental bread is explained. About A.D. 401–21.

1 The manner of their elders and priests administering the flesh and blood of Christ unto the church; and they administered it according to the commandments of Christ; wherefore we know the manner to be true; and the elder or priest did minister it—

2 And they did kneel down with the church, and pray to the Father in the name of Christ, saying:

3 O God, the Eternal Father, we ask thee in the name of thy Son, Jesus Christ, to bless and sanctify this bread to the souls of all those who partake of it; that they may eat in remembrance of the body of thy Son, and witness unto thee, O God, the Eternal Father, that they are willing to take upon them the name of thy Son, and always remember him, and keep his commandments which he hath given them, that they may always have his Spirit to be with them. Amen.

Book of Mormon, Moroni Chapter 5:

The mode of administering the sacramental wine is set forth. About A.D. 401–21.

1 The manner of administering the wine—Behold, they took the cup, and said:

2 O God, the Eternal Father, we ask thee, in the name of thy Son, Jesus Christ, to bless and sanctify this wine to the souls of all those who drink of it, that they may do it in remembrance of the blood of thy Son, which was shed for them; that they may witness unto thee, O God, the Eternal Father, that they do always remember him, that they may have his Spirit to be with them. Amen.

There are very few set prayers in The Church of Jesus Christ of Latter-day Saints. The sacrament prayers are two of them. We must stand up for the Lord, always remember Him, and keep his commandments. If we do that, we will have His Spirit to be with us. With our Lord's Spirit with us, we can defeat fear, avoid slavery, and gain the strength to use our intelligence to avoid sin. We can become like God and our Savior, Jesus Christ. When we recite the sacrament prayers, we remember that the Lord gave up His life and bled at every pore to atone for our sins and draw us to Him. As we think, we are reminded by the sacrament prayers that we are eternal beings along with the Lord, and this Earth is our classroom for part of our eternal journey. We can and must overcome fear and govern our lives by intelligence, not emotion. When the Prophet Joseph Smith was unjustly imprisoned in Liberty Jail in Missouri under the very real threat of being killed by his enemies, he prayed to the Lord for deliverance. Here is part of the answer that the Lord gave Joseph, found in Section 122 of the Doctrine and Covenants:

Doctrine and Covenants, Section 122:

4 And although their influence shall cast thee into trouble, and into bars and walls, thou shalt be had in honor; and but for a small moment and thy voice shall be more terrible in the midst of thine enemies than the fierce lion, because of thy righteousness; and thy God shall stand by thee forever and ever.

5 If thou art called to pass through tribulation; if thou art in perils among false brethren; if thou art in perils among robbers; if thou art in perils by land or by sea;

6 If thou art accused with all manner of false accusations; if thine enemies fall upon thee; if they tear thee from the society of thy father and mother and brethren and sisters; and if with a drawn sword thine enemies tear thee from the bosom of thy wife, and of thine offspring, and thine elder son, although but six years of age, shall cling to thy garments, and shall say, My father, my father, why can't you stay with us? O, my father, what are the men going to do with you? and if then he shall be thrust from thee by the sword, and thou be dragged to prison, and thine enemies prowl around thee like wolves for the blood of the lamb;

7 And if thou shouldst be cast into the pit, or into the hands of murderers, and the sentence of death passed upon thee; if thou be cast into the deep; if the billowing surge conspire against thee; if fierce winds become thine enemy; if the heavens gather blackness, and all the elements combine to hedge up the way; **and above all, if the very jaws of hell shall gape open the mouth wide after thee, know thou, my son, that all these things shall give thee experience, and shall be for thy good.**

8 The Son of Man hath descended below them all. Art thou greater than he?

9 Therefore, hold on thy way, and the priesthood shall remain with thee; for their bounds are set, they cannot pass. Thy days are known, and thy years shall not be numbered less; therefore, fear not what man can do, for God shall be with you forever and ever. (Emphasis Added)

We do not get to choose the lessons our Heavenly Father and Jesus Christ want us to learn during our mortal journey. Joseph Smith prayed for deliverance in 1839 from Liberty Jail, and he was delivered. Many important truths were revealed through Joseph from 1839 to 1844. The Lord was delivered from execution by Jewish leaders for a time, as recorded in the New Testament, John 10:30 – 39; but that did not mean our Lord was released from his mission to atone for our sins by giving his life when the time came. It was Joseph Smith's mission to usher in the dispensation of the fullness of times and restore the ancient Church of Christ. When the time came, Joseph Smith sealed his testimony of our Savior with his blood when he was murdered by a mob in Illinois at Carthage Jail on June 27, 1844.

Many of our Heavenly Father's children in our time have given their lives, and continue to give their lives, in testimony that God lives, that Jesus is the Christ, that the ancient Gospel of Jesus Christ has been restored to Earth in preparation for our Lord's return, and that we are children of the living God. With the testimony of Jesus in our hearts, and a firm determination to endure to the end, fear will never govern our lives. We will never become slaves in mortality. We must not fear to read the Book of Mormon, because it is proof that we live in the last days before the return of our Savior. Understanding the messages revealed to us in the Book of Mormon will assist us to make the preparations we must make to prepare for our Lord's return.

Chapter Eight

Follow the Spirit

*Acting upon divine revelation will **always** benefit us on our mortal journey, no matter how hard following revelation may seem at the time received.*

The Book of Mormon is proof that our Heavenly Father has commenced the work of preparing the Earth for the return of His son in great power and glory to fulfill all prophecy since the beginning of the world. In its concluding chapter we find in Moroni 10:3-5 the promise that the Holy Ghost will reveal the truth of the Book of Mormon to us under the conditions stated. But if we are to benefit from our lives in mortality, we must learn to follow the Spirit. Having the Spirit bear witness to us that the Book of Mormon contains the Word of God will do us little good if we fail to act on the revelation we receive. Or as the Apostle James instructed in the New Testament:

James Chapter 1:
22 But be ye doers of the word, and not hearers only, deceiving your own selves.

23 For if any be a hearer of the word, and not a doer, he is like unto a man beholding his natural face in a glass:

24 For he beholdeth himself, and goeth his way, and straight-way forgetteth what manner of man he was.

25 But whoso looketh into the perfect law of liberty, and con-tinueth therein, he being not a forgetful hearer, but a doer of the work, this man shall be blessed in his deed.

The great challenge for each of us is to learn during our lifetimes to recognize the Spirit of the Lord when revelation comes to us. Once we recognize the Spirit, we must obey and act on the revelation we receive. Knowledge comes from personal experience combined with revelation and spiritual confirmation. No person will get it right every time, but if we pay attention in class while we are alive in our Heavenly Father's classroom we call Earth, and act on the revelation received, we can get better and better at recognizing and obeying the Spirit. Acting upon divine revelation will *always* benefit us on our mortal journey, no matter how hard following revelation may seem at the time received. What follows in this chapter are some of the experiences I have had with following the Spirit of revelation. To my regret, I have not always listened and acted upon revelation from God. But when I have, I have always been blessed.

The Lord blessed me with good parents. My father was not devoted to organized religion, but he attended our Methodist Church with my mother and participated as best he could. My father, however, had many spiritual experiences in his life and had strong faith in the Lord. I will share three of his spiritual experiences here that were very important to him and helped shape the remainder of his life.

My Dad, Roscoe Tate's, first experience with the Spirit that he shared with me was when he, as a teenager, was helping his father operate a sawmill near the family's farm close to Dahlonega, Georgia. There was an accident and the power saw nearly cut Roscoe's leg off at the knee. The first problem was to stop the bleeding and save his life. Roscoe's grandfather, my great grandfather, Thomas Abraham Pearson Tate, had one of the gifts of the spirit – he could stop bleeding. Although he was not at the sawmill, people were able to notify Tom Tate very quickly, and he asked the Lord to stop the bleeding immediately. The bleeding stopped. Stopping the bleeding saved Roscoe's life and his leg ultimately healed. However, Roscoe lost an entire year of school while his leg healed; and he carried a huge scar on almost his entire knee for the remainder of his long life. That experience as a teenager gave Roscoe knowledge that the Lord lived and that there was real power in the Spirit.

My grandfather, Emory Tate, moved his family to South Georgia during Roscoe's last couple of years of high school. Roscoe was able to finish his secondary education at a small community college in Douglas, Georgia. The depression was taking hold in those days and times were hard. Roscoe was able to find work at a mechanic's shop on Saturdays and after school to help make ends meet. My Dad was a good mechanic, even as a very young man, and they called him "Doc" at the shop where he worked part-time. One Friday afternoon while Roscoe was working after school, the shop foreman was approached by the full-time mechanic who worked next to where Roscoe worked. The mechanic told the foreman that he had been working on one car for two days trying to fix the brakes and could not figure out how to fix them. This car had mechanical, not hydraulic, brakes. The shop foreman told the mechanic: "Stop working on the car. I will have "Doc" take a look at the car tomorrow (Saturday) morning when he comes in.

That Friday night my Dad dreamed that the problem with the brakes was broken motor mounts. Every time the driver pushed the brake pedal, the engine would lift, and the brakes would not engage the wheels. When Dad came in to work Saturday morning, the shop foreman asked Roscoe to look at the car the mechanic next to him had been working on for the past two days. Roscoe got down under the engine and asked the mechanic to press the brake pedal. Sure enough, the engine lifted - the motor mounts were broken. Dad told the mechanic to fix the motor mounts and that would fix the brake problem. The mechanic immediately became very angry. He accused my Dad of knowing all along what was wrong with the brakes and failing to share his knowledge of how to fix the car. The full-time mechanic was ready to fight right then.

Roscoe was shocked at the mechanic's behavior and told the mechanic the truth – that he had dreamed the night before what was wrong with the brakes. Dad's explanation just made matters worse. The mechanic did not believe Dad and accused him of being a liar. The shop foreman had to break up the conflict so that work could continue in the shop. That night Roscoe had another dream. He was told by a Heavenly

Messenger that this was a lesson for him: "Do not cast your pearls before swine."

After that my Dad was very reluctant to discuss his spiritual experiences unless he knew he was speaking with those whom he was sure were believers. We find the scripture that Roscoe's messenger quoted in the New Testament at the conclusion of what we refer to as the Sermon on the Mount; and also the same words in the Lord's instructions to the Nephites as recorded in the Book of Mormon:

Matthew Chapter 7:

6 ¶ Give not that which is holy unto the dogs, neither cast ye your pearls before swine, lest they trample them under their feet, and turn again and rend you.

Book of Mormon 3 Nephi Chapter 14:

6 Give not that which is holy unto the dogs, neither cast ye your pearls before swine, lest they trample them under their feet, and turn again and rend you.

That same revelation was also given to the Prophet Joseph Smith, as recorded in the Doctrine and Covenants:

Doctrine and Covenants, Section 41:

6 For it is not meet that the things which belong to the children of the kingdom should be given to them that are not worthy, or to dogs, or the pearls to be cast before swine.

The third spiritual experience my father related to me occurred in Shanghai, China, in the mid 1930's. My Dad was what we now refer to as a "China Marine." He spent most of his four-year Marine enlistment in Shanghai. During that period, there was also a large Japanese troop presence in Shanghai. When U.S. Marines went into Shanghai for leave, there were often fights, some serious, between Marines and Japanese troops also on leave. On one occasion while on leave in Shanghai, my Dad and Marines with him were in a bar when a group of Japanese troops came in. Soon things started to get out of hand, and my Dad told his companions that they had better go back to the U.S. base. Just as they left the bar, my father had the strong feeling that he should take a different route to the base because the Japanese intended to ambush him and his friends. He knew that the Lord was warning him, so he heeded the Spirit and changed his route. As they rounded a corner on the alternate route, they were able to see in the distance Japanese troops waiting to attack them. Recognizing the Spirit and acting on the revelation received saved the day for those Marines.

The first encounter with the Spirit that I recall was when, as a child of about 6 years old, my appendix ruptured. I remember very little from that age, but I still remember vividly the pain I felt. Our family physician referred us to Emory University Hospital in Atlanta, and I remember a moment of cold soberness as I was being wheeled into the operating room. I somehow knew that I was about to die, and I did not want to die. I told my Father in Heaven in silent prayer that if he would let me live, I would serve him during my life. At age 34, I made the decision to be baptized a member of The Church of Jesus Christ of Latter-day Saints. The memory of that promise I made as a child came vividly back to me just before I stepped into the waters of baptism. However, I have felt the inspiration of the Spirit throughout my life, and have tried, not always successfully, to keep the promise I made at age 6.

I am convinced that everyone receives direction from the Spirit. My marriage was a gift of spiritual guidance. The first date I had with Sharon was at Rock Eagle 4-H Center in Eatonton, Georgia. I was a freshman at Georgia Tech going to college while working in Jacksonville, Florida, on the co-op plan. My younger brother, Albert Tate, was competing for State honors in his 4-H project. I drove down to Georgia's Rock Eagle 4-H Center to support him. When I arrived at Rock Eagle, our DeKalb County 4-H Extension Agent, Thomas Helton, came up to me. Sharon had already graduated from college and was a 4-H extension agent working with young women in Cobb County, Georgia. Both Sharon and I were National 4-H winners in our respective projects and were both from DeKalb County – so I knew her well. Thomas said to me: "Jim, you need to ask Sharon out on a date tonight, because one of the other 4-H extension agents is pursuing her and she doesn't like him." I replied, "Tom, she is too old for me." He replied: "No, she is not too old for you. Just do it."

Sharon and I had a date that night, and on the way back home the next day, the Spirit revealed to me that Sharon was to be my wife. I remember telling my mother as soon as I got home that Sharon and I would be married, and she said: "Have you asked her yet?" I replied that I had not asked her, but I knew that we would be married. It took me another two years to convince Sharon to marry me. What finally made it happen was when my Dad came up to me and said: "Son,

I think you should marry Sharon. If you will marry her, I will pay your tuition and college expenses for your last year at Georgia Tech, and assist with your living expenses if you need help." I count winning Sharon as my wife my greatest gift in this life next to finding out that Jesus the Christ is my Savior; and I am a son of the living God. It was following the Spirit that gave me the courage to pursue her hand.

After Sharon and I married, during my last year at Georgia Tech, I decided to go to law school. My degree would be in chemical engineering; and my idea was to become a patent attorney. One of my classmates had followed this route and encouraged me to apply to George Washington University Law School in Washington, D.C. for their night program. There were companies that would hire engineers and pay their tuition for law school. I was admitted by George Washington Law for their night program and hired by DuPont to work in their patent legal department in Washington, D.C. DuPont also agreed to pay my law school tuition. When I told my Dad my plan, he said: "Son, forget law school. It is time you went to work." I was very happy that DuPont had agreed to hire me and pay law school tuition. With Sharon and I both working, I knew we would be just fine financially.

When I started law school, the Vietnam War was raging, and I was at risk of being drafted. I did not mind serving my Country, but I wanted to finish my education. I would no longer be a full-time student and eligible for student deferment after I left Georgia Tech. I prayed about what to do and felt that I should write my draft board a letter. In that letter, I explained that I could not afford to attend law school full-time, but by taking 10 hours each semester and 8 hours each summer, I could stay even with full-time law students from September to September each year. I promised the draft board that when I finished law school I would go into the service. Although my draft board in Georgia never agreed to defer me, my deferment continued each year as I sent them my transcripts.

For my last year of law school, George Washington offered me a scholarship to attend full-time. At that point Sharon and I had sufficient savings to enable me to leave DuPont. We had also started a successful business with a partner, Steve Cram, selling women's hair pieces. In May 1968 I graduated from George Washington University Law School with a Juris Doctor degree at the same time as the full-time law students that started law school with me in September 1965. Now I had, what was for me, a very important decision to make – would I keep my promise to the Georgia draft board and go into the service?

The above background is to explain how it was that I became an officer in the United States Army assigned to the Chemical Corps, decided to follow the Spirit, and ended up with the 101st Airborne Division in Vietnam. When I finished law school, I was married and too old to be drafted under the then existing laws and policies. I did not feel a very strong push to go into the service, but somehow I just knew that I had to keep my word to the Georgia draft board. Since I had a degree in chemical engineering, I applied for a direct commission in the Army as a chemical officer. My application was granted, and I received a commission as a Second Lieutenant in the United States Army. I was sent to Anniston, Alabama, for basic officer training. Upon completion of basic, the Army personnel office assigned me to the U.S. Army Materiel Command (AMC) at Baileys Crossroads, in Northern Virginia – within walking distance of the apartment where Sharon and I lived. I was one of two active-duty patent attorneys in the United States Army; and had the thought that the Lord was really looking after me.

After working at AMC for a few months, I had the strong feeling that I needed to get back in the top physical shape that I had attained in basic training. I felt the inspiration came from our Lord, so I immediately started to work. By early 1969, I was in great shape and happy that I listened to the Spirit. It did not occur to me that perhaps there was another reason I needed to get back in shape. One day as I was working at AMC, a flyer, with a distribution list, was put on my desk with the information that civilians were urgently needed to volunteer to serve in Vietnam. I looked at the flyer and sent it on since I was an active-duty soldier – not a civilian. As soon as that flyer left my desk I had the overwhelming feeling, an almost physical sensation, that I had to immediately volunteer for service in Vietnam. I had never in my life had such a strong feeling about anything.

Days passed and I could not shake the feeling. Sharon was busy with our business partner running our business and I helped whenever I could. It was insane to think that I should voluntarily go to Vietnam. I did not feel that I could tell anyone about how I felt, so I went across the Potomac River to the National Cathedral in Washington and prayed to the Lord to take away the feeling that I needed to volunteer for Vietnam. That prayer did not work – the feeling persisted, and if anything became more intense.

I decided to obey. I sent a letter to my commander, who was a 4-star general commanding AMC. I soon received word back that my request for duty in Vietnam was denied. Instead, I would be sent to Detroit to work with the Germans on intellectual property issues with the new main battle tank. I knew that overruling a 4-star would not be easy, so I decided to write to the Commander in Chief – the President of the United States. I sent recently elected President Richard Nixon a letter explaining that my commander had denied my request to serve in Vietnam and asked the President to overrule the 4-star's decision. Within a week of sending that letter, orders came for me to report to the 101st Airborne Division in Vietnam.

As soon as the orders for Vietnam came, I felt I had a duty to the Army in case I was killed to make sure my family knew I had volunteered. I spoke to my Dad, swore him to secrecy, and told him the truth. I could not tell Sharon, because I was afraid she would be furious that I was abandoning her. It took me over twenty more years to get the courage to tell Sharon what I had done. At this time, when he learned I had orders for Vietnam, my younger brother, Al Tate, who was also in the Army serving in the United States, contacted the Army and volunteered to go to Vietnam in my place. There was a government policy not to send all children in one family into a combat zone. I was married; Al was not married, and he thought he had a good argument to take my place. The Army finessed that one somehow without telling my family that I volunteered. My little brother and I had not agreed on very many issues up to that point in our lives, but we were still close. His attempt to take my place in Vietnam touched my heart then and brings tears to my eyes as I write this.

When I stepped off the airplane in early August 1969 at Bien Hoa Airbase near Saigon, Vietnam, it was just like stepping into a furnace. On my first night in Vietnam, I was given a pack, a rifle, and ammunition and sent to guard the perimeter at the base. I remember looking up at the stars and making this statement: "Heavenly Father, I don't have to be in this place. I must be the dumbest of all your sons." How wrong I was in making that statement.

My service in Vietnam helped me learn to overcome fear; and that one lesson has been of immense benefit to me during my life. My service in Vietnam shaped my career; and is the reason I have one of my two wonderful daughters. Sharon had difficulty carrying a child to term, and we decided to adopt a Vietnamese orphan. Not long after making the decision to adopt, Sharon became pregnant with Virginia, who was born in the spring of 1974. Sharon and I decided to follow through with adoption, and in October 1974, I returned to Vietnam and adopted Devon, who was about three months old when I carried her on the plane departing Saigon. Ginny and Devon were practically twins growing up; and have been very close friends during their lives. Their love and support for each other has been a great joy to their mother and me.

The sequel to my Vietnam service occurred a few months after I returned from my trip to adopt Devon. I received a call from a friend who had worked on my political campaigns assisting with press matters. He had just read a news wire report originating in Da Nang, South Vietnam, that Ed Daly, President and owner of World Airways, was stuck on a runway with a load of orphans. The U. S. State Department would not let Ed Daly take off and bring orphans to the United States. Knowing that I had just returned from Vietnam, my friend wanted to know if there was anything I could do.

From that call came The Emergency Committee to Save the Babies to get the orphans out of Vietnam ahead of the communist advance southward. My friend and business associate, Bob Raley, had gone to Vietnam with me to adopt an orphan, and he became co-chair. The actor, Yul Brynner, had also adopted a little girl from Vietnam; and I asked him to be co-chair. Yul was a friend of President Gerald Ford, and we needed Yul to enlist the President's help. I was a member of the Virginia House of Delegates at the time, and asked my colleague, Wyatt Durette, to also co-chair our committee. Virginia's Governor, Mills Godwin, was also a friend and we soon had a powerful group of supporters. AT&T donated 10 watts lines (in those days very valuable assets), and local merchants fed our hundreds of volunteers.

Shortly after learning that Ed Daly was stuck on a Da Nang runway, Bob Raley and I took our babies with us and held a press conference in my Vienna, Virginia, office building. Among press attending were network TV reporters from New York. At that press conference I announced that Ed Daly was not being allowed to take off and save the orphans. I gave out the telephone number of the relevant State Department official. Soon afterwards I received a call from the State Department official. He said: "Jim, call off the dogs. We will let the plane take off." Later President Ford went to California to welcome one of the planes carrying orphans. United Airlines called me and volunteered to fly orphans with escorts provided by United to final destinations at no charge. Virginia's agency that supervised adoptions sent a team to our office to screen adoptive families. In my wildest dreams I could never have predicted that following the message from the Spirit to volunteer for service in Vietnam could have the impact that it ultimately had.

As I conclude this chapter, I want to share a couple of extremely personal, spiritual, experiences that a friend, Craig, had while also serving in Southeast Asia while the Vietnam War was in progress. I am not including Craig's last name, because his experiences are very private and sacred to him. When the angel descended from Heaven, holding the golden plates of the Book of Mormon in his hand, to show the Three Witnesses to the Book of Mormon - Oliver Cowdery, Martin Harris, and David Whitmer - we learn that angels can carry heavy gold. Obviously, there are real forces at work in our lives that involve the Spirit that we cannot explain and do not understand. Our lack of understanding does not make the spiritual forces less real. Understanding the Spirit of the Lord only comes spirit to spirit – we must have faith in our Lord Jesus Christ, obey His commandments, and act without fear on the spiritual revelation we receive.

I first heard Craig tell of his experiences in Southeast Asia in the mid 1980's. I was a member of the High Council of the Annandale Virginia Stake of The Church of Jesus Christ of Latter-day Saints. Craig had been given a special assignment from our Annandale Virginia Stake President that required Craig to work closely with the High Council. We became friends. Craig was a pilot in the Air Force and was serving as military aide to the Vice President. When Craig's assignment in Washington was over, he was reassigned to a new duty station. On his last Sunday, Craig's Bishop asked him to be the principal sacrament meeting speaker. I was present when Craig gave his talk and was amazed to hear him tell how the Lord had saved his life on two occasions in very dramatic ways.

After the meeting was over, I went up to Craig and said: "Craig, you have been in Washington for a number of years, why are you just now sharing your experiences?" Craig replied that if he told what happened to him at the beginning of a new assignment, he would be asked to retell his experiences over and over during the entire time he lived in that community.

Craig went to California for his new work assignment; and I later received a Church calling to work with youth. Craig's experiences were so powerful, that I wanted him to come back to Washington and teach our youth about the power of the Spirit. Subsequently I was called to serve as a Bishop, a member of a Stake Presidency, and as a member of the Washington D.C. North Mission Presidency. While serving in each assignment, I tried without success to get Craig to come back and repeat the farewell talk he had shared when he left the Annandale Virginia Stake. Finally, during my last year serving in the Washington D.C. North Mission Presidency, about twenty years after I heard Craig tell of his experiences in Southeast Asia, Craig changed his mind.

Craig came back to Washington when he learned that I had been called to serve as President of the Alabama Birmingham Mission of The Church of Jesus Christ of Latter-day Saints, and he must have had some sympathy for me.

At the time Craig agreed to come back to Washington, one of my assignments as a Counselor to the Washington D.C. North Mission President was to work with the Washington D.C. Temple Visitors Center of The Church of Jesus Christ of Latter-day Saints. Every third Sunday evening we held a "Why I Believe Fireside" in the 500 plus seat auditorium at the Visitors Center; and I invited Craig to come and speak as our featured speaker. He agreed to fly from California to speak to us. Although it was not our practice to record fireside events, I asked and received permission from Bill Marriott, the presiding authority in our area at the time, to record Craig's talk.

During the three years I served as Mission President in the Alabama Birmingham Mission, I served with hundreds of young missionaries and dozens of senior missionaries. Every six weeks we would have "transfers", and missionaries going home would spend the night at the mission home. We would have a program, and after all was over, I would show the missionaries the video of Craig's talk at the Washington D.C. Visitors Center given in the fall of 2006. Craig is an officer, a gentleman, and a faithful member of The Church of Jesus Christ of Latter-day Saints. Not many years after his assignment as military aid to the Vice President, General Norman Schwarzkopf, commander of Operation Desert Storm, asked Craig to come to the Middle East and assist in training pilots that would be part of Desert Storm. Craig was trusted at the highest levels of the United States government and military. We can have confidence that Craig is telling the truth about what happened to him in Southeast Asia, and about the revelations that led up to those experiences.

As I write this in 2022, the President of The Church of Jesus Christ of Latter-day Saints is Russell M. Nelson. At the time Craig was preparing to leave home to enter pilot training in the Air Force during the Vietnam War, President Nelson was Craig's Stake President. One day Craig received a message that President Nelson wanted to speak with him. During their interview, President Nelson told Craig that he felt that before Craig left for duty in the Air Force, he should go through the Temple. In those days an exception from the President of the Church was required for a person in Craig's situation to attend the Temple. President Nelson told Craig that he wanted Craig to finish his pilot training and come back through Salt Lake City on his way to Southeast Asia. President Nelson had secured permission from the First Presidency of the Church for Craig to go through the Temple on condition that Craig continue to obey our Lord's commandments.

After finishing pilot training, Craig came back to his home in Salt Lake City, obtained the recommends necessary to go through the Temple, and received his Temple ordinances as President Nelson had asked him to do. While at the Temple, Craig met the Temple President, who later sent him a letter that Craig received after arriving at his duty station in Southeast Asia. In the letter, the Temple President said that he had been praying for Craig, and it was revealed to him that if Craig would obey the Lord's commandments, his life would be preserved; and when he returned from the war, he would receive a wife chosen by the Lord.

In Southeast Asia, Craig was assigned to fly special missions and work with a group of native people who were resisting the communists. One day Craig was asked to test a plane that had been in maintenance. As Craig and another pilot flew together over the mountains, antiaircraft fire hit Craig's plane, blew off the front and destroyed his engine. His radio stilled worked, and he had some control over his elevation but little or no control over his rudder. He radioed his companion flying nearby and asked him to call in the medivac chopper to pick up the pieces. Craig was not wearing a parachute. All was very quiet - except for the sound of wind whistling around him. Just as Craig's plane started to lose altitude and head for the side of a mountain, Craig thought about the letter he had received from the Salt Lake Temple President and said in his mind: "Well, I guess he got that wrong." Instantly, an overwhelming feeling of calm came over Craig, and the next thing he remembered was standing on the side of the mountain. Parts of his plane were all around him, and one foot was on part of the plane's instrument panel. Craig survived the crash of his plane into the side of the mountain with very little injury.

Enemy soldiers began shooting and Craig ran zig zag down the mountain. A rescue helicopter saw Craig and picked him up; but that chopper was hit, and Craig and the rescuers had to autorotate and land. Another chopper then came in and carried Craig and the first chopper's crew to safety.

Craig's next miracle that occurred during his military service in Southeast Asia happened not long after his plane crashed. It seems that sometimes when the Lord performs a miracle on the Earth, he wants to make sure there is no doubt that he always delivers on his promises. I am sure Craig had no doubts about the miracle of his surviving the plane crash; but his survival of the overrun of his firebase was no less a miracle. Craig's firebase was in the middle of a volcanic crater that had natural defensive advantages. However, one night an enemy determined to drive the U.S. out of that area of Southeast Asia attacked and overran the base. Craig called in air support from Thailand and two F-4's responded. They were able to get below the cloud cover and started circling the base above the rim of the dormant volcanic mountain. Craig was in radio contact with the senior pilot and was asked where Craig wanted them to put the ordinance. By that time, Craig could see the enemy soldiers coming right at him and told the pilots to put it right on top of them. The first ordinance that hit blew away Craigs radio and most of his shelter. The second pilot could not contact Craig and asked his senior pilot where to put his load of CBU bombs. The senior pilot told his junior to put his load where the senior pilot had dropped. CBU stands for cluster bomb units, and soon literally thousands of mini bombs were headed right at Craig. Flares were lighting up the sky and Craig could see the bomb coming without any change of angle – which meant the CBU's were coming right at him.

In the meantime, enemy soldiers reached Craig. He had saved one bullet in his pistol for himself, but instead used it to kill the first enemy soldier to get to him - who then fell on top of Craig. The first soldier's buddy then pointed his rifle at Craig's head and pulled the trigger. The bullet went around the inside of Craig's helmet and out the back, and the injury to Craigs head was not life threatening. At that point the CBU's hit and killed everyone nearby – except Craig. The enemy soldier who fell on top of Craig absorbed the bomb fragments that would otherwise have killed Craig. Craig reported that he just laid back against what was left of his shelter and shook until the rescue forces came in the next day.

Craig's experiences with the power of God remind me of the constancy of God. David and Goliath, Daniel and the lions' den, and Shadrach, Meshach, and Abednego in the furnace, really happened – just as recorded in the Old Testament. Moses really displayed His power to Pharoh just as recorded; and Moses led the ancient Israelites through the Red Sea on dry land, just as recorded in scripture. God is the same today as He was yesterday; and will be the same tomorrow. If miracles cease, it is because we lose faith and ignore our Heavenly Father's commandments. The professor who no longer believes the Bible and those who deny God and glory in their own wisdom notwithstanding, God still lives, Jesus is the Christ, and miracles like those that happened to Craig still occur in our day. Chapter 7 of Moroni in the Book of Mormon states the Spiritual laws that govern miracles and is reproduced in **NOTE 15** in the Appendix (Page 230).

Chapter Nine

A Bible! A Bible! We Have Got a Bible, and There Cannot Be Any More Bible

A doctrine that tries to shut the mouth of God can only come from the devil himself. It is truly sad that many have been taken in by Lucifer's sophistry and have refused to read the Book of Mormon with an honest heart, with real intent, and then ask our Heavenly Father in the name of Jesus Christ for spiritual confirmation of its truth. God has promised his children that the Holy Ghost will testify of the truth of the Book of Mormon, and God does not lie.

Entering politics, meeting many wealthy and powerful people, and working hard to do my best as a public servant eventually led me to be baptized a member of The Church of Jesus Christ of Latter-day Saints. I became convinced that I had my ladder leaning on the wrong wall: Pursuit of power, prestige, and wealth would not lead to happiness. Since becoming a member of our Lord's Restored Church, established in our time to prepare for the Second Coming, I have been blessed to meet many of our Lord's sons and daughters who are successful in every sense and are also happy. I was led by the Spirit to the Lord's Restored Church by first paying attention to advice from our Lord as recorded in the New Testament at the conclusion of the Sermon on the Mount. Here is the scripture:

Matthew Chapter 7:

15 ¶ Beware of false prophets, which come to you in sheep's clothing, but inwardly they are ravening wolves.

16 Ye shall know them by their fruits. Do men gather grapes of thorns, or figs of thistles?

17 Even so every good tree bringeth forth good fruit; but a corrupt tree bringeth forth evil fruit.

18 A good tree cannot bring forth evil fruit, neither can a corrupt tree bring forth good fruit.

19 Every tree that bringeth not forth good fruit is hewn down, and cast into the fire.

20 Wherefore by their fruits ye shall know them.

21 ¶ Not every one that saith unto me, Lord, Lord, shall enter into the kingdom of heaven; but he that doeth the will of my Father which is in heaven.

22 Many will say to me in that day, Lord, Lord, have we not prophesied in thy name? and in thy name have cast out devils? and in thy name done many wonderful works?

23 And then will I profess unto them, I never knew you: depart from me, ye that work iniquity.

*24 ¶ **Therefore whosoever heareth these sayings of mine, and doeth them, I will liken him unto a wise man, which built his house upon a rock:***

25 And the rain descended, and the floods came, and the winds blew, and beat upon that house; and it fell not: for it was founded upon a rock.

26 And every one that heareth these sayings of mine, and doeth them not, shall be likened unto a foolish man, which built his house upon the sand:

27 And the rain descended, and the floods came, and the winds blew, and beat upon that house; and it fell: and great was the fall of it.

28 And it came to pass, when Jesus had ended these sayings, the people were astonished at his doctrine:

29 For he taught them as one having authority, and not as the scribes. (Emphasis Added).

I observed that of all groups of people that I knew, members of The Church of Jesus Christ of Latter-day Saints best fit the Savior's description of His people. I was not stopped from reading the Book of Mormon because I believed that the Bible was all the word of God that we needed. When I finally determined that the path I was taking in life would not lead me to happiness no matter how "successful" I became, I was willing to read the Book of Mormon with real intent as Moroni directed. However, during my service as a mission president, I learned that many people will not read the Book of Mormon because they think that the Bible itself bans additional scripture. The Lord was rejected by most of the Jews during his mortal ministry, so we should not be surprised that most have rejected the Book of Mormon and the Lord's Restored Church in our day.

Bill Marriott is a well-known member of The Church of Jesus Christ of Latter-day Saints. I first met Bill through his childhood friend, Bill Ingersoll. Bill and Carolyn Ingersoll helped me in my political campaigns and were friends. They were examples of doers of the Word. I will never forget attending the funeral of J. Willard Marriott, Bill Marriott's father, and founder of the Marriott Corporation. At the time of his father's death, Bill Marriott was the President of the Washington D.C. Stake of The Church of Jesus Christ of Latter-day Saints. He conducted his father's funeral, but the presiding official at that funeral was Ezra Taft Benson, President of The Church of Jesus Christ of Latter-day Saints. I was President Benson's daughter's Bishop at the time. I remember looking up at the podium at the front of the church, in the summer of 1985, at the Washington D.C. Stake Center and seeing President Benson, former President Richard Nixon, evangelist Billy Graham, and other very important people. I also remember that during his remarks President Benson turned to Billy Graham after we had just sung *How Great Thou Art* and said to him: "I have always loved that hymn. I made up my mind that if I ever had anything to do with it, I would make sure that hymn got into our hymn books. I do, and it is." It is unfortunate that leaders of other faiths have not grown to love the Book of Mormon, as President Benson loved *How Great Thou Art*. If leaders of other faiths would just read the Book of Mormon with an honest heart and real intent, they would grow to love it and want their members to have the same experience. The Book of Mormon, like the Bible, contains the words of Jesus Christ. As it says on its cover, the Book of Mormon is "Another Testament of Jesus Christ."

Despite the efforts of the Marriott Corporation (placing copies of the Book of Mormon in hotel rooms), and millions of full-time and member missionaries of The Church of Jesus Christ of Latter-day Saints, most people professing to be Christians have not, and apparently will not, read the Book of Mormon. Many of these same people who will not read the Book of Mormon believe that we are living in the last days before the Second Coming of Jesus Christ; but they do not believe in modern revelation, or that there can be scripture in addition to the Bible. When Utah U.S. Senator Orrin Hatch learned that I had been called to be President of the Alabama Birmingham Mission, he brought to my attention the 29th Chapter of 2nd Nephi in the Book of Mormon. The Lord's ancient prophet in America had foreseen the coming forth of the Book of Mormon in our day and the resistance it would face. Senator Hatch had faced the "Closed Canon" resistance to the Book of Mormon while serving as a young missionary in Ohio. Proponents of the closed canon cite as support a scripture from the Bible, found in the last verses of the New Testament:

Revelations Chapter 22:

18 For I testify unto every man that heareth the words of the prophecy of this book, If any man shall add unto these things, God shall add unto him the plagues that are written in this book:

19 And if any man shall take away from the words of the book of this prophecy, God shall take away his part out of the book of life, and out of the holy city, and from the things which are written in this book.

Senator Hatch wrote a book about the "closed canon" and pointed out that essentially the same language is found in the Old Testament in the Book of Deuteronomy:

Deuteronomy Chapter 4:

2 Ye shall not add unto the word which I command you, neither shall ye diminish ought from it, that ye may keep the commandments of the Lord your God which I command you.

It seems obvious that John the Revelator was telling his readers not to alter the words that he received from God, and Moses was doing the same. Neither Prophet was saying that they intended to muzzle the Lord. If Moses was really proclaiming a closed canon in Deuteronomy, we would be missing most of the Bible, including the words of our Savior and his Apostles. We would also be missing Isaiah, Jeremiah, Daniel, and the other prophets of the Old Testament. The Bible did not exist as a Book when John wrote Revelation, so those verses could not possibly apply to the Bible as "this book," but only to the Book of Revelation. Many of the books in the Bible are believed to have been written after the Book of Revelation, so they would have been banned as well.

It was not long after I arrived in Alabama that I learned that the doctrine of the *Closed Canon* was alive and well. Thanks to Senator Hatch's book, I was ready for the challenge when it came.

Two young sister missionaries were assigned to work the neighborhoods closest to the mission home where Sharon and I lived. One day while out proselytizing the sisters found a professor who taught at a nearby protestant university. His position at the university was Chair of the Divinity School. No one graduated from that curriculum without the professor's blessing. The sisters invited the professor to have a missionary discussion and asked if he would like to have the discussion with their Mission President joining with them. The professor accepted and the lesson was scheduled to be given in the mission home. I made sure that we had a King James Version of the Bible and a "Triple" for the professor to use during our lesson. The *Triple* contained the Book of Mormon, The Doctrine and Covenants, and the Pearl of Great Price with the Articles of Faith of The Church of Jesus Christ of Latter-day Saints at the end. As I recall, the professor showed up at the mission home about noon, and his first name was Tom. I liked him right away and respected him for his courage in accepting the invitation from our missionary sisters.

After spending about a half hour getting to know each other, we got right into our lesson. The professor was young (compared to me) and obviously very intelligent. He knew his Bible. At the first opportunity as the lesson progressed, he looked right at me and said: "What about the closed canon?" Although Senator Hatch's book had alerted me to the issue and how to answer his questions, I decided to take a little different path with the professor. I said: "Tom, I am a lawyer by profession. Although we think of the Lord as a carpenter, I happen to believe that the Lord is also a very good lawyer. The Lord himself prepared an answer to your question concerning the closed canon 2500 years ago." That answer got the professor's attention; and I could see the curiosity in his face. He wanted to know what the Lord had to say about the doctrine of the closed canon.

I asked Tom to turn in the Book of Mormon to 2nd Nephi Chapter 29 and read out loud to all of us what the Lord had to say about the doctrine that there could never be scripture in addition to the Bible. Here is what Tom read from the Book of Mormon:

Book of Mormon, 2nd Nephi Chapter 29

Many Gentiles will reject the Book of Mormon—They will say, We need no more Bible—The Lord speaks to many nations— He will judge the world out of the books which will be written. About 559–545 B.C.

1 But behold, there shall be many—at that day when I shall proceed to do a marvelous work among them, that I may remember my covenants which I have made unto the children of men, that I may set my hand again the second time to recover my people, which are of the house of Israel;

2 And also, that I may remember the promises which I have made unto thee, Nephi, and also unto thy father, that I would remember your seed; and that the words of your seed should proceed forth out of my mouth unto your seed; and my words shall hiss forth unto the ends of the earth, for a standard unto my people, which are of the house of Israel;

3 And because my words shall hiss forth—many of the Gentiles shall say: A Bible! A Bible! We have got a Bible, and there cannot be any more Bible.

4 But thus saith the Lord God: O fools, they shall have a Bible; and it shall proceed forth from the Jews, mine ancient covenant people. And what thank they the Jews for the Bible which they receive from them? Yea, what do the Gentiles mean? Do they remember the travails, and the labors, and the pains of the Jews, and their diligence unto me, in bringing forth salvation unto the Gentiles?

5 O ye Gentiles, have ye remembered the Jews, mine ancient covenant people? Nay; but ye have cursed them, and have hated them, and have not sought to recover them. But behold, I will return all these things upon your own heads; for I the Lord have not forgotten my people.

6 Thou fool, that shall say: A Bible, we have got a Bible, and we need no more Bible. Have ye obtained a Bible save it were by the Jews?

7 Know ye not that there are more nations than one? Know ye not that I, the Lord your God, have created all men, and that I remember those who are upon the isles of the sea; and that I rule in the heavens above and in the earth beneath; and I bring forth my word unto the children of men, yea, even upon all the nations of the earth?

8 Wherefore murmur ye, because that ye shall receive more of my word? Know ye not that the testimony of two nations is a witness unto you that I am God, that I remember one nation like unto another? Wherefore, I speak the same words unto one nation like unto another. And when the two nations shall run together the testimony of the two nations shall run together also.

9 And I do this that I may prove unto many that I am the same yesterday, today, and forever; and that I speak forth my words according to mine own pleasure. And because that I have spoken one word ye need not suppose that I cannot speak another; for my work is not yet finished; neither shall it be until the end of man, neither from that time henceforth and forever.

10 Wherefore, because that ye have a Bible ye need not suppose that it contains all my words; neither need ye suppose that I have not caused more to be written.

11 For I command all men, both in the east and in the west, and in the north, and in the south, and in the islands of the sea, that they shall write the words which I speak unto them; for out of the books which shall be written I will judge the world, every man according to their works, according to that which is written.

12 For behold, I shall speak unto the Jews and they shall write it; and I shall also speak unto the Nephites and they shall write it; and I shall also speak unto the other tribes of the house of Israel, which I have led away, and they shall write it; and I shall also speak unto all nations of the earth and they shall write it.

13 And it shall come to pass that the Jews shall have the words of the Nephites, and the Nephites shall have the words of the Jews; and the Nephites and the Jews shall have the words of the lost tribes of Israel; and the lost tribes of Israel shall have the words of the Nephites and the Jews.

14 And it shall come to pass that my people, which are of the house of Israel, shall be gathered home unto the lands of their possessions; and my word also shall be gathered in one. And I will show unto them that fight against my word and against my people, who are of the house of Israel, that I am God, and that I covenanted with Abraham that I would remember his seed forever.

When Tom, the chair at the divinity school, finished reading 2ⁿᵈ Nephi 29, he was obviously very impressed – I almost used the word "touched." That was the last we heard about the closed canon from Tom. We departed on good terms; and I later learned that Tom left his university and continued his education at the University of Alabama at Tuscaloosa. The fact is that the Lord is a good lawyer – a powerful advocate for the true Gospel of Christ, and his points are very persuasive to those who will listen with an open mind and honest heart. A doctrine that supposes that the God of the Universe cannot give his children more scripture cannot be correct. Or, as the Lord made the point in verses 9, 10, and 11 of 2nd Nephi 29 above:

> *9 And I do this that I may prove unto many that I am the same yesterday, today, and forever; and that I speak forth my words according to mine own pleasure. And because that I have spoken one word ye need not suppose that I cannot speak another; for my work is not yet finished; neither shall it be until the end of man, neither from that time henceforth and forever.*
>
> *10 Wherefore, because that ye have a Bible ye need not suppose that it contains all my words; neither need ye suppose that I have not caused more to be written.*
>
> *11 For I command all men, both in the east and in the west, and in the north, and in the south, and in the islands of the sea, that they shall write the words which I speak unto them; for out of the books which shall be written I will judge the world, every man according to their works, according to that which is written.*

A doctrine that tries to shut the mouth of God can only come from the devil himself. It is truly sad that many have been taken in by Lucifer's sophistry and have refused to read the Book of Mormon with an honest heart, with real intent, and then ask our Heavenly Father in the name of Jesus Christ for spiritual confirmation of its truth. God has promised his children that the Holy Ghost will testify of the truth of the Book of Mormon, and God does not lie.

As I write this, I now recall an interview with one of our young missionaries serving near Birmingham. He was frustrated that so many people in his area had been convinced by their preachers that the Book of Mormon was a tool of the devil. This young man wanted to print copies of 2nd Nephi 29 and distribute it to homes in his area. I did not let him do it, because I thought that people could perceive his doing so as an attack on the Bible. Nevertheless, the young man had a valid point; and I should have given our missionaries special training in how to use our Lord's answer to the closed canon doctrine.

When Sharon and I were almost finished with our three-year tour presiding over the Alabama Birmingham Mission, we received an invitation to attend a concert at one of the nearby mega Protestant churches. Several of our members were performing in their orchestra and they invited us to come hear them play and enjoy the concert. I did not want to go, because I knew that the church involved was antagonistic to The Church of Jesus Christ of Latter-day Saints, and even had a special Sunday School class that trashed our Lord's Church. However, when I learned that the concert program consisted of many of the arrangements prepared by Mack Wilberg, Music Director of the Tabernacle Choir at Temple Square, I decided to attend. Those attending with us, all in Sunday dress with missionary tags, were several senior missionary couples and my two Assistants to the President

(AP's). We sat down together and filled up two or three rows near the front on the right side of the chapel.

It really was a great concert, and I was grateful to our local members for inviting us. When the concert ended, our host minister (who had a PhD) came to the front of the raised platform and said a few words. The preacher closed with this remark: "What a wonderful concert! You know, the Lord can send us revelation through music." When he said those words, it was just like the Lord sent a bolt of lightning through my very soul. I hardly heard the words of the closing prayer that the preacher offered. As soon as he said "Amen", I got up from my seat and walked up to the preacher – who was not far away. I climbed up 2 or 3 of the 6 or so steps to reach the platform and the preacher walked over to me. Our missionaries knew something was afoot and followed me.

I thanked the preacher for inviting us to his concert and related how much we enjoyed the music. I then told the preacher that he was absolutely right – God could send revelation to man via music in our time. I then said these words: "And God can also send us revelation of the Word of God." His reaction to my words could best be described as a reaction one would have to being slapped across the face with gloves and challenged to a duel. That preacher lit into me like we would say in the South – a guinea after a June bug. I knew that I had to end the conversation immediately. I could not confront that preacher on his own turf. I thanked him again and we left. When we reached the car, Sharon scolded me. She said: "You ought to be ashamed of yourself causing trouble with that preacher in his own church."

By the time I reached the Mission Home, which was a few minutes away, I was feeling really bad. I immediately sat down and typed a letter to that preacher. I told him that I did not mean to cause contention in his church and repeated how much we enjoyed his concert. I then took the letter to the local Post Office just before midnight and mailed the letter. Two days later the preacher responded to my letter. He thanked me for coming, acknowledged the contributions of Mack Wilberg, and then proceeded to defend the indefensible. For at least a page he argued in his letter that God could no longer reveal scripture and words to man. Truly in his church we had a case of the blind leading the blind.

I want to end this chapter by referring to the declaration of another professor that did not understand that he was a child of the living God. I am going to name this professor, because I have not read his publications and want readers if so advised to be able to do their own research on the professor's thinking. Professor Thomas Altizer was an Associate Professor at Emory University in Atlanta for over a decade. He held a Ph.D. in history of religions from the University of Chicago. In the mid 1960's while I was attending law school, Professor Altizer proclaimed that God was dead. He was featured more than once in Time Magazine and appeared on the Merv Griffin Show to a national audience – where he was given time to repeat his previous declarations that God is dead. Such a declaration in the 1960's took a great deal more courage than a similar announcement would today. Those who claim today, as prophesied in the Book of Mormon, that there cannot be another Bible are really claiming that God is dead and is unable to give his children on Earth any additional direction on how we should live our lives.

Those who imagine that man has the power to muzzle our Heavenly Father and our Savior literally have been blinded and are unable to see their own potential to become joint heirs with Jesus Christ. They have imagined up for themselves a God and Savior that do not exist. Not only are they fulfilling the prophecy of 2nd Nephi Chapter 29 in the Book of Mormon; they are fulfilling a prophecy given by the Apostle Paul in a letter to Timothy as recorded in the New Testament:

2nd Timothy Chapter 4

1 I charge thee therefore before God, and the Lord Jesus Christ, who shall judge the quick and the dead at his appearing and his kingdom;

2 Preach the word; be instant in season, out of season; reprove, rebuke, exhort with all longsuffering and doctrine.

3 For the time will come when they will not endure sound doctrine; but after their own lusts shall they heap to themselves teachers, having itching ears;

4 And they shall turn away their ears from the truth, and shall be turned unto fables.

I have not done a study of just which religious leaders gave Professor Altizer the roughest time for declaring that God is dead; but will wager that such a study will find that those who would muzzle God today come from the same groups that found a declaration that God is dead so abhorrent and directed their ire against Professor Altizer decades ago.

Chapter Ten

Sacrifice- A Principle of the Gospel

The law of sacrifice has been in effect throughout the ages. It is the faith to obey and accept the consequences that matters, not whether our lives are preserved in mortality.

Sacrifice is a principle of the Gospel of Jesus Christ. Our Heavenly Father sacrificed His Son for us so that justice could be satisfied when we are forgiven for our sins on condition of repentance. Jesus also explained that His sacrifice was to demonstrate the love of God for His children and instill in us a desire to follow Jesus and obey His commandments. Abraham was chosen by God to be the father of the faithful. In order for Abraham to understand the agony our Heavenly Father and our Savior would suffer in carrying out the plan of salvation, Abraham was required by God to sacrifice his son, Isaac. At the last minute, an angel saved Isaac's life, but Abraham was obedient, not knowing Isaac would be spared.

The Savior bled from every pore as he suffered in the Garden of Gethsemane for our sins and prayed that His coming sacrifice could be waived, but then said "Nevertheless, thy will be done." When Jesus' disciples realized that Jesus was telling them He must die, they objected to His death; but the Savior explained to them that His sacrifice must proceed, and that Satan was putting those objections into their hearts. Had the Savior shrunk from His atoning sacrifice, the plan of salvation would have been thwarted and Satan would have rejoiced.

We are not all required to sacrifice our mortal lives in order to reach our potential. But in all ages, some of our Heavenly Father's children have been required to give their lives. In all ages, all true followers of our Savior have been required to be obedient and sacrifice their wealth and lives if commanded to do so.

A dispensation of the Gospel is a time when God reveals truth anew to man on Earth. There was a dispensation in Adam's time, a dispensation in Abraham's time, a dispensation in Moses' time, and a dispensation when our Savior came to Earth to live out His mortal life. The dispensation at the time Jesus walked the Earth is called the Dispensation of the Meridian of Time. The dispensation of our time is called the Dispensation of the Fullness of Times. The United States of America was established by inspiration from God to be a place of religious freedom to allow the Dispensation of the Fullness of Times to begin in preparation for the return of Jesus Christ in power and great glory. Our dispensation began when our Heavenly Father and Jesus Christ called another Prophet in our time – the young boy, Joseph Smith, Jr. Just three years after organization of The Church of Jesus Christ of Latter-day Saints and publication of the Book of Mormon, Joseph received this revelation about sacrifice:

Doctrine and Covenants Section 97:

7 The ax is laid at the root of the trees; and every tree that bringeth not forth good fruit shall be hewn down and cast into the fire. I, the Lord, have spoken it.

8 Verily I say unto you, all among them who know their hearts are honest, and are broken, and their spirits contrite, and are willing to observe their covenants by sacrifice—yea, every sacrifice which I, the Lord, shall command—they are accepted of me.

9 For I, the Lord, will cause them to bring forth as a very fruitful tree which is planted in a goodly land, by a pure stream, that yieldeth much precious fruit.

In our dispensation, the Dispensation of the Fullness of Times, we are required to humble ourselves and make every sacrifice that the Lord shall command us to make. In what are now called the Lectures on Faith, in Lecture 6:7, the principle was taught this way: *A religion that does not require the sacrifice of all things, never has power sufficient to produce the faith necessary unto life and salvation.*

The law of sacrifice has been in effect throughout the ages. It is the faith to obey and accept the consequences that matters, not whether our lives are preserved in mortality. Abinadi, the Book of Mormon Prophet, was burned at the stake, but the Prophet Alma, who watched his execution, was spared. Those taught by the Prophets Alma and Amulek were destroyed by fire; but Alma and Amulek were spared. The

Lord himself was spared on occasion but was later crucified. The journey that results from following the plan of salvation begins with desire. Desire leads to faith. Faith leads to obedience. Obedience brings knowledge, which leads to power, eternal life, and salvation.

In the Book of Mormon the Prophet, Alma, explained how the process of conversion works in Alma, Chapter 32, which is included in the Appendix, **NOTE 16** (Page 236).

In Chapter 32 Alma turned from preaching to those who were well off with this world's goods to those that were poor. Alma acknowledged that it was better to accept the Gospel without being compelled by poverty to do so, and that there were also those who were not poor that would seek for truth and accept it when preached to them. Rich or poor, once the journey looking for salvation begins with true humility and desire, the process is the same. We can begin, as the process is described in Alma Chapter 32, by merely having a desire to learn the truth. If we will follow up with that desire, as set forth in the scripture, we will harvest the fruit of eternal life, the most desirable of all fruit.

We have a record in the New Testament of a young man coming to the Lord for instruction. Jesus told the young man to sell what he had, give to the poor, and follow him - if he did that, he would have eternal life. The young man went away with sorrow in his heart, because he was very wealthy and unwilling to part with this world's goods. It is a tragedy of our time that many people not only refuse to make sacrifices of worldly goods to follow the Savior - they will not give of their time or change their lives when the Savior knocks.

Some may consider that obeying the law of tithing is a sacrifice. However, I have been surprised at how few people who are investigating The Church of Jesus Christ of Latter-day Saints object to, and question, the law of tithing. I have at times thought that the seemingly ready acceptance of the law of tithing is because missionaries do a good job of teaching the basis for giving ten percent of our increase to the Church. Here are the applicable scriptures – first, from the next to last chapter of the last book of Old Testament; second, from the Doctrine and Covenants of The Church of Jesus Christ of Latter-day Saints:

Malachi Chapter 3:

7 ¶ Even from the days of your fathers ye are gone away from mine ordinances, and have not kept them. Return unto me, and I will return unto you, saith the Lord of hosts. But ye said, Wherein shall we return?

8 ¶ Will a man rob God? Yet ye have robbed me. But ye say, Wherein have we robbed thee? In tithes and offerings.

9 Ye are cursed with a curse: for ye have robbed me, even this whole nation.

10 Bring ye all the tithes into the storehouse, that there may be meat in mine house, and prove me now herewith, saith the Lord of hosts, if I will not open you the windows of heaven, and pour you out a blessing, that there shall not be room enough to receive it.

11 And I will rebuke the devourer for your sakes, and he shall not destroy the fruits of your ground; neither shall your vine cast her fruit before the time in the field, saith the Lord of hosts.

12 And all nations shall call you blessed: for ye shall be a delightsome land, saith the Lord of hosts.

During the first years of the Dispensation of the Fulness of Times, in which we now live, the Prophet Joseph Smith received instructions from the Lord about tithing. At the time of this revelation, there was no clear definition of tithing. In Section 119 of the Doctrine and Covenants, the Lord required members to give their surplus property to their Bishop, and thereafter to pay 10% of their increase annually. Today the law of tithing means to pay ten percent of our increase annually. In the decades that I have been a member of The Church of Jesus Christ of Latter-day Saints, I have never seen a collection plate passed. When I was a Methodist, a collection plate was passed every Sunday and lay leaders tried to visit families once each year to collect annual pledges. Members of The Church of Jesus Christ of Latter-day Saints bring their tithes to the Bishop without being asked, and in a few countries today are able to pay on-line. Here is the scripture:

Doctrine & Covenants Section 119:

3 And this shall be the beginning of the tithing of my people.

4 And after that, those who have thus been tithed shall pay one-tenth of all their interest annually; and this shall be a standing law unto them forever, for my holy priesthood, saith the Lord.

I have personal knowledge that obeying the law of tithing brings blessings, both temporal and spiritual. However, if a man or woman goes into the Bishop, pays tithing, and then goes out in the Church parking lot and wishes he or she had put a down payment on a car they want, that person might just as well go back in and get his tithing payment back and keep the money. That payment of tithing will not do them one bit of good.

We must pay our tithing with a heart that says: "I am so happy to give this little bit of money to help build our Lord's Kingdom on Earth in preparation for his return." If we pay our tithing with a willing heart, the Lord will look after us. I now believe that the reason I have observed so much acceptance of the law of tithing by investigators of the Church is because the Spirit of the Lord bears witness to their spirits that tithing is a true principle. When I was investigating The Church of Jesus Christ of Latter-day Saints, I was impressed that tithing and other donations went directly to expenses and not to salaries of preachers. Local and regional leaders of the church serve without pay of any kind, and they rejoice at the privilege. Every member is invited to learn the Gospel of Jesus Christ and then teach others out of love.

For a recent sacrament meeting in our home congregation, the Bishop had asked those preaching that Sunday to speak about sacrifice. One of the speakers looked out at me and recalled a missionary lesson that I was asked to attend with him and the missionaries. They taught the lesson in the Chapel, and I met them there on the way home from my office. I had totally forgotten the occasion but remembered the lesson when the speaker said this: "Brother Tate asked the investigator why he was interested in The Church of Jesus Christ of Latter-day Saints and told him that it is not an easy church to be a part of." The speaker said he was surprised that

I would say that to a person just beginning his investigation of the Church. In the Lord's Restored Church, established to prepare for the Second Coming, everyone is expected to do his or her part in running the Church and in preaching the Gospel. That means each member, not just the Bishop and his counselors, must first learn the Gospel. That is a lifelong process not to be taken lightly.

While serving as President of the Alabama Birmingham Mission, I was constantly asked by missionaries to assist in answering questions that investigators, and sometimes even members, posed to them. Many questions about Church doctrine had to do with what is commonly called the "Word of Wisdom." It is widely known that faithful members of The Church of Jesus Christ of Latter-day Saints do not use tobacco or alcohol and do not drink coffee or tea. It is said that when early critics of The Church of Jesus Christ of Latter-day Saints first learned about the revelation that the Prophet Joseph Smith received that is called the "Word of Wisdom" they said: *Now we know for sure that Joseph Smith is a false prophet. He is right about liquor, but everybody knows that tobacco is good for you.*

As time has passed, science and medicine have caught up with revelation and tobacco is today widely accepted as a substance that is harmful to take into our bodies. However, other parts of the revelation containing the Word of Wisdom are still controversial. Committing to live the Word of Wisdom is a requirement for baptism as a member of The Church of Jesus Christ of Latter-day Saints; so, I made a sincere effort to learn all I could about the subject and the sacrifices those who wanted to be baptized would have to make to comply.

Here is the revelation, with historical headnote, known as "The Word of Wisdom:"

Doctrine and Covenants Section 89

Revelation given through Joseph Smith the Prophet, at Kirtland, Ohio, February 27, 1833.

As a consequence of the early brethren using tobacco in their meetings, the Prophet was led to ponder upon the matter; consequently, he inquired of the Lord concerning it. This revelation, known as the Word of Wisdom, was the result. 1–9, The use of wine, strong drinks, tobacco, and hot drinks is proscribed; 10–17, Herbs, fruits, flesh, and grain are ordained for the use of man and of animals; 18–21, Obedience to gospel law, including the Word of Wisdom, brings temporal and spiritual blessings.

1 A Word of Wisdom, for the benefit of the council of high priests, assembled in Kirtland, and the church, and also the saints in Zion—

2 To be sent greeting; not by commandment or constraint, but by revelation and the word of wisdom, showing forth the order and will of God in the temporal salvation of all saints in the last days—

3 Given for a principle with promise, adapted to the capacity of the weak and the weakest of all saints, who are or can be called saints.

4 Behold, verily, thus saith the Lord unto you: In consequence of evils and designs which do and will exist in the hearts of conspiring men in the last days, I have warned you, and forewarn you, by giving unto you this word of wisdom by revelation—

5 That inasmuch as any man drinketh wine or strong drink among you, behold it is not good, neither meet in the sight of your Father, only in assembling yourselves together to offer up your sacraments before him.

6 And, behold, this should be wine, yea, pure wine of the grape of the vine, of your own make.

7 And, again, strong drinks are not for the belly, but for the washing of your bodies.

8 And again, tobacco is not for the body, neither for the belly, and is not good for man, but is an herb for bruises and all sick cattle, to be used with judgment and skill.

9 And again, hot drinks are not for the body or belly.

10 And again, verily I say unto you, all wholesome herbs God hath ordained for the constitution, nature, and use of man—

11 Every herb in the season thereof, and every fruit in the season thereof; all these to be used with prudence and thanksgiving.

12 Yea, flesh also of beasts and of the fowls of the air, I, the Lord, have ordained for the use of man with thanksgiving; nevertheless they are to be used sparingly;

13 And it is pleasing unto me that they should not be used, only in times of winter, or of cold, or famine.

14 All grain is ordained for the use of man and of beasts, to be the staff of life, not only for man but for the beasts of the field, and the fowls of heaven, and all wild animals that run or creep on the earth;

15 And these hath God made for the use of man only in times of famine and excess of hunger.

16 All grain is good for the food of man; as also the fruit of the vine; that which yieldeth fruit, whether in the ground or above the ground—

17 Nevertheless, wheat for man, and corn for the ox, and oats for the horse, and rye for the fowls and for swine, and for all beasts of the field, and barley for all useful animals, and for mild drinks, as also other grain.

18 And all saints who remember to keep and do these sayings, walking in obedience to the commandments, shall receive health in their navel and marrow to their bones;

19 And shall find wisdom and great treasures of knowledge, even hidden treasures;

20 And shall run and not be weary, and shall walk and not faint.

21 And I, the Lord, give unto them a promise, that the destroying angel shall pass by them, as the children of Israel, and not slay them. Amen.

Note that when this revelation was initially given to the Prophet Joseph Smith, the Lord gave it as advice, not by commandment. Subsequently, obedience to parts of Section 89 – abstaining from tobacco, alcohol, and hot drinks (interpreted as coffee and tea) - was made mandatory for members.

It took me ten years from my first missionary lesson with missionaries referred by Professor Cliff Fleming to be baptized a member of The Church of Jesus Christ of Latter-day Saints. During the period immediately before I made the decision to become a member and on numerous occasions since I was baptized, I have had personal experiences with the Word of Wisdom, and I know that it is of divine origin. Although the Word of Wisdom is just one of the principles taught by the Lord to his followers in preparation for His return, I know that it is a very important principle that will lead us closer to the Lord. I have also learned that obeying the Word of Wisdom may seem like a sacrifice, but in truth living the Word of Wisdom is a great blessing. However, despite the over four decades that have passed since I became a member of The Church of Jesus Christ of Latter-day Saints, I still have much to learn about the revelation from God found in Section 89 of the Doctrine and Covenants.

The first experience I had with the Word of Wisdom was to test its divine origin and relationship to the truth of the Restored Gospel of Jesus Christ. Not long before my baptism, I was drinking too much alcohol. I don't believe Sharon knew how serious my problem was, because I seemed to function normally, and she never said anything to me about my drinking. Nevertheless, I knew I had an alcohol problem, and I knew it was serious. Missionaries were visiting us every week, sometimes more often. They had a series of lessons they needed to get through and I did not make it easy for them. Elders David Buhler and Tom Hoopes were resourceful in finding answers to my questions and did not hesitate to ask newly elected Senator Orrin Hatch from Utah for his help. Elder Buhler had worked hard on Senator Hatch's campaign and knew him well.

My recollection is that in the order of lessons taught at that time, the lesson on the Word of Wisdom was near the end of the required lesson series, and it was getting to be time for me to "fish or cut bait" as the saying goes. By this time the Spirit had already born witness to me that the Book of Mormon was the Word of God. I felt that Joseph Smith must be a true Prophet of God. It followed that The Church of Jesus Christ of Latter-day Saints must be the Lord's true Church, set up by the Lord himself to prepare a people for the return of our Savior. Nevertheless, because of my pride I knew I would resist baptism because of the Church's position on African Americans holding the Priesthood. I was in a pickle and did not know what to do. I decided to test the Lord.

One early morning after working out, showering, and getting ready for work I found a quiet place to be alone and pray. I knelt down and prayed vocally as the missionaries taught, and as the Prophet Joseph Smith prayed immediately before our Heavenly Father and our Savior, Jesus Christ, appeared to him for the first time. I still remember the exact words of my prayer. I prayed: "Heavenly Father, if there is anything to this Church that I am investigating, I want you to take away my desire for alcohol. In the name of Jesus Christ, Amen." No bolt of lightning hit me after my prayer, and no angel or other Heavenly Personage paid a visit to me. However, that evening as it came time for me to have a drink, I had absolutely no desire to even take a taste. Since that prayer until now as I write this, I have not desired alcohol in any form nor taken a drink of alcohol in any form. The Lord passed the test and I have been blessed by that prayer and its answer for decades. Obeying the Word of Wisdom for me has not been a sacrifice, it has been a great blessing.

My next experience with the Word of Wisdom came a few years later. This experience concerned another part of the Word of Wisdom that is not a part of missionary lessons, nor is it well understood by most people – and I include in "most people" members of The Church of Jesus Christ of Latter-day Saints. The advice given to us by the Lord in Doctrine and Covenants Section 89 is not all mandatory; but like obedience to the command to abstain from tobacco and alcohol, obedience to the remainder of the revelation in Section 89 is not really a sacrifice but is instead a blessing. Only verses 5-9 relate to tobacco, alcohol and hot drinks (coffee and tea). The remaining verses are in three additional categories: the introduction to Section 89; advice on what we should eat; and promises that come from obedience. Advice on what we should and should not eat led to my next experience with the Word of Wisdom. That experience was how I learned that there is a lot more to our Lord's revelation in Section 89 than meets the eye.

About 6 or 7 years after becoming a member of The Church of Jesus Christ of Latter-day Saints, my parents came up from Jekyll Island, Georgia, where they lived as retired "Senior Citizens," to spend Thanksgiving with us in Northern Virginia. The year prior to their visit my mother, Alberta Henderson Tate, had been diagnosed with breast cancer and had been through a mastectomy, chemotherapy, and radiation. That same year I had taken my father, a retired civil engineer, with me on a business trip to Seattle to meet a client who was also a civil engineer. This client was working on a new material to use in the construction of roads, and I thought my Dad would be interested in what was being developed – since he had designed many of the Interstate Highways in Georgia. After the Seattle visit, my Dad, Roscoe Tate, and this engineer began to call each other quite often and discuss the new technology.

One evening the Seattle engineer, whose name I believe was Bill, called when Roscoe was away at his hunting club. He had gotten to know my mother via the phone, and upon learning that my father was not home, proceeded to chat with her. Finally, Bill said: "Alberta, you seem depressed. What is the matter?" My mother replied: "Bill, I have cancer, and I have just learned that the mastectomy, chemotherapy, and radiation did not work, and my cancer has come back. I am not going to suffer through another round of chemotherapy and radiation. I am getting ready to die, and I am depressed about it." Bill replied and said: "Alberta, you do not have to die from cancer. I am a survivor of pancreatic cancer – which is usually fatal. I will send you a book." When my mother received the book from Bill, it looked familiar to her. It turned out that Alberta's book of the month club had featured the book and it was on her bookshelf – but she had never read it.

Alberta received Bill's book in late August. It was a how to survive cancer book written by married professors at a midwestern university who had met and been instructed by a Japanese American named Micho Kushi. My mother was a retired high school teacher who taught Latin in a school district in the suburbs of Atlanta. She was very bright and put her whole effort into following the instructions in the book she received from Bill. The details about what to eat and how to eat were very specific in Bill's book; and my mother followed them strictly. By the time Thanksgiving arrived and her visit with us in Virginia, the following had occurred:

1. Mother had lost a lot of weight and looked great.

2. Her oncologist in Savannah, at her last medical checkup, said this to her: "Alberta, your blood work is normal – no sign of cancer. I don't know what you are doing, but you must share with me what is working for you. My sister has cancer like you have, and I cannot help her."

As we sat at the Thanksgiving dinner table next to each other, I watched my mother eat and she watched me eat. I was eating meat and potatoes. Mother was eating brown rice, vegetables, a special soup, and chewing her food thoroughly. She was also watching me eat. She said: "Son, the way you eat is not healthy." As I had been watching mother eat, it hit me that she was following scripture in the "what we should eat" portion of Doctrine and Covenants Section 89. I replied: "Mother, I know that the way you are eating is good, because we have several verses that describe what you are doing in our scriptures. If you will give me information about your book, I will order a copy and read it."

From that Thanksgiving dinner and events that followed, I ended up traveling to Brookline, Massachusetts to meet with Michio Kuchi. I subsequently did some legal work for him. He was a founder of the macrobiotic movement and many people have been blessed by following his advice. Michio asked me how I knew that the macrobiotic way of eating was a good thing. I replied that I was a member of The Church of Jesus Christ of Latter-day Saints, and we had a scripture that described what he was teaching. He asked me to read the scripture to him. I then read Section 89 of the Doctrine and Covenants to Michio. When I finished reading, he said: "Read it to me again." I read Doctrine and Covenants Section 89 again. Then Michio said: "That is macrobiotics."

I have a friend who retired as a well-known defense official. Upon retirement, he was hired by a major airline to help the company overcome difficult problems it was having. Not long after getting this new job, he was called to be a leader in The Church of Jesus Christ of Latter-day Saints in an area where he knew practically no one. He was a busy man, but during his whole life he had been successfully managing difficult situations. Then my friend, I will call him Ron, learned that he had cancer and would require immediate surgery. The surgery would alter the person he was. His wife said to him: "Ron, this will not be you. Let's look for another way." Their search led Ron to follow a regimen similar to that given by the Lord in Section 89. Ron is a very disciplined person and followed the nutrition protocol strictly. The cancer did not spread; and he avoided the radical surgery.

While serving as a mission president, the question I most often received concerning the Word of Wisdom was about coffee and tea. I grew up in the deep South and drank a lot of sweet tea – probably close to a freight train load before I was baptized a member of The Church of Jesus Christ of Latter-day Saints. However, I never liked and never drank coffee. The chief investigator in my law practice was an old Marine and former policeman. He was addicted to coffee, and lots of it. After decades of drinking coffee, he developed chronic headaches. His doctor told him that if he wanted to end the headaches, he would have to stop drinking coffee and other caffeinated beverages. It took months, but Jim was finally able to kick the coffee habit and sure enough, after more time, his headaches mostly went away. Giving up coffee was not an easy thing for Jim, but his headaches were worse than the pain of giving up coffee.

Now imagine a couple of young missionaries who are teaching a man who is in the same position my law firm's investigator was in – addicted to lots of coffee – but has no discernable health problems that have resulted from his drinking coffee. The man, call him Paul, has been reading the Book of Mormon, and has felt good about what he is learning from his reading and from meeting with the missionaries. He has attended church a few times with his missionaries and is thinking about baptism. Knowing that Paul loves his coffee, Paul's missionaries have been reluctant to give him the lesson on the Word of Wisdom and bring to his attention that before he can be baptized, he must stop drinking coffee. Like most missionaries who are teaching people investigating the Restored Church, they love Paul and do not want to drive him away by teaching a principle – no coffee or tea – that they themselves may not really understand. They have no idea if Paul will be willing to sacrifice his coffee to become a member of The Church of Jesus Christ of Latter-day Saints. The missionaries decide to ask their mission president (in this case me) if there is a health reason requiring that prospective members give up coffee and tea.

I have been asked the question many times why members of The Church of Jesus Christ of Latter-day Saints are prohibited from drinking coffee and tea. When I became a mission president, I was forced to focus my thoughts and prayers on the issue much more closely than I had done in the past. One thought I had was that if a person was not willing to make such a small sacrifice as giving up coffee to become part of the Kingdom of God on Earth, then the Lord did not want them in His Kingdom. It was a thought that came to me, and I knew immediately that I needed to repent. If our Heavenly Father loves us enough to send his Son to die for us, we should love His children, our brothers and sisters, enough to help them overcome addictions - whatever those addictions may be. Remembering the difficult and painful ordeal my legal investigator went through overcoming his addiction to coffee helped me to put myself in the shoes of those with addictions who are investigating the Church.

However, sharing my investigator's experience with headaches, and Jim's doctor's order to stop drinking coffee did not really answer the missionaries' question about a medical reason for not drinking coffee. It is my habit to listen to a news radio station that serves the Washington D.C. area while I am working out in the mornings. Every few months there is a report on research about the health effects of drinking coffee. Health effects of drinking wine are also a regular subject for comment as different studies are commissioned by various interested parties and make the news. During one news cycle it was reported that drinking coffee in moderate amounts is very beneficial for health and will prolong life. A few months later research showed that drinking coffee, and even moderate amounts of wine is not a healthy thing to do. I concluded that there is not a health answer to the missionaries' question about the Word of Wisdom. I had a great aunt that lived past one hundred years and was self-sufficient almost until she died. She lived in the mountains of Georgia, way out in the country. She was grossly overweight and grew and smoked her own tobacco. By just about any health standard that I am familiar with, my great aunt should never have made it to old age – much less 100 years old. During her long life, she was rarely ill. After reflecting on the question asked by the missionaries, I answered by telling them to just trust the Lord and not worry about finding a health explanation for the Word of Wisdom.

It is true that medical research has been able to document the adverse health effects of tobacco; and thereby answer those who smugly said during the nineteenth century that Joseph Smith was a false prophet because everybody knew that tobacco was good for you. Early members of the Church, who were the pioneers that sacrificed so much to build the foundation of our Lord's Restored Church, were not deterred by critics in those days, and we must not be swayed in our time. We must live by faith and every word that proceeds from the mouth of God as delivered to us by ancient and living prophets. Our eternal salvation cannot be based on information we receive from scientists, physicians, and social scientists whose understanding will certainly change as they gain more knowledge. We follow the Word of Wisdom not because science recommends it, but because the Lord expects it.

In ancient times the Syrian Captain, Naaman, had leprosy. A Jewish servant in his household shared her knowledge that there lived a prophet in Israel who could cure his disease. Naaman's pride almost prevented him from following instructions from Elisha, the Lord's prophet in those days, but Naaman repented and was cured. We would do well to follow Naaman's example, repent of our pride and follow the Lord's prophets in our time. The scriptural account of Naaman's experience is found in the Old Testament, 2 Kings 5, reproduced in **NOTE 17** in the Appendix (Page 241).

It is not given to mortal man to understand all things. To this day we don't understand how people are healed by the spirit, but I know for a fact that healing can and does come via the Spirit of the Lord. We do not understand scientifically how Naaman was healed after washing himself seven times in the Jordan River; or how Elisha's servant contracted leprosy because of his greed and deceit. However, if we are faithful and endure to the end, the time will come when we can learn the truth of all things.

In the last chapter of the Book of Mormon we are promised that if we will read the Book of Mormon with an honest heart and real intent, if we ask Him the Lord will reveal the truth of the Book of Mormon to us by the power of the Holy Ghost. But that is not all we are promised in the three verses I am referring to – we are promised in verse 5 that the Holy Ghost will reveal to us the truth of *all* things. Here is the scripture from the Book of Mormon:

Moroni Chapter 10

3 Behold, I would exhort you that when ye shall read these things, if it be wisdom in God that ye should read them, that ye would remember how merciful the Lord hath been unto the children of men, from the creation of Adam even down until the time that ye shall receive these things, and ponder it in your hearts.

4 And when ye shall receive these things, I would exhort you that ye would ask God, the Eternal Father, in the name of Christ, if these things are not true; and if ye shall ask with a sincere heart, with real intent, having faith in Christ, he will manifest the truth of it unto you, by the power of the Holy Ghost.

5 And by the power of the Holy Ghost ye may know the truth of all things.

If we exercise faith, and act on that faith, we can know that the Book of Mormon is true; that Joseph Smith was chosen by the Lord to be his Prophet to restore the ancient Church of Jesus Christ with ancient Priesthood power; that the Book of Mormon is proof that our Heavenly Father is preparing to send his Son once again to the Earth in great glory, and that no sacrifice is so great as to prevent us from embracing the Restored Gospel and doing our part to prepare for our Savior's return. It is only by first exercising faith and acting on that faith without fear that we will be able to reach our full potential as sons and daughters of the living God. The Lord is the same today as He was in ancient times. He is knocking and we need to let Him in.

The Prophet Moroni spelled out our duty in words written by him especially for us who are called to come to Earth in the last days before our Heavenly Father sends again his Son – this time in great glory. In the Book of Mormon, Moroni Chapter 9, the Prophet makes clear that the Lord is constant throughout the ages, and if miracles cease, or gifts of the spirit cannot be found, it is because we are not worthy of them. Moroni Chapter 9, verses 7-30 is set forth in **NOTE 18** in the Appendix (Page 244).

Chapter Eleven

Living Prophets

For thousands of years our Heavenly Father has sent prophets to instruct His children. People have consistently rejected living prophets who are able to able to provide revelation in real time. These are the last days before the Second Coming, and it is time we started listening to our Lord's prophets so we can prepare for the return of our Savior.

On an early spring day in 1820, the fourteen-year-old boy, Joseph Smith, went into the woods near his home in upstate New York to pray to his Heavenly Father. Young Joseph had been reading his Bible and read in the New Testament, in the book of James, that if a person lacked wisdom, he could ask God and receive an answer. Here is the scripture:

James Chapter 1

5 If any of you lack wisdom, let him ask of God, that giveth to all men liberally, and upbraideth not; and it shall be given him.

6 But let him ask in faith, nothing wavering. For he that wavereth is like a wave of the sea driven with the wind and tossed.

7 For let not that man think that he shall receive any thing of the Lord.

8 A double minded man is unstable in all his way.

Joseph's prayer, our Heavenly Father's and Jesus Christ's answer, and subsequent events led to the Restoration of the Aaronic Priesthood on May 15, 1829, when Joseph Smith and Oliver Cowdery were baptized and received the lesser Priesthood from the resurrected John the Baptist. Sometime between the visit of John the Baptist and the organization of The Church of Jesus Christ of Latter-day Saints on April 6, 1830, in Fayette, New York, Joseph and Oliver received the Melchizedek Priesthood near the Susquehanna River from the resurrected Apostles of our Lord: Peter, James, and John. Regardless of which date is chosen – 1820, 1829 or 1830, the absolute knowledge of mortal man has expanded exponentially since the restoration of the Priesthood and the organization of our Lord's Restored Church.

One of the requirements laid down by the Lord and recorded in scripture, is that the Gospel must be preached to all living on the earth before the Lord returns in power and great glory to reign. In 1831, when the Restored Church was in its infancy, the Lord made it clear to His living prophet that the Gospel had to be preached to everyone:

Doctrine and Covenants Section 58:

64 For, verily, the sound must go forth from this place into all the world, and unto the uttermost parts of the earth—the gospel must be preached unto every creature, with signs following them that believe.

65 And behold the Son of Man cometh. Amen

After giving the commandment to preach to the whole world, the Lord proceeded to inspire His children to provide the necessary means to make that possible. Never before in recorded history has knowledge and revelation been sent from Heaven at such a rapid rate. Now missionaries can travel to the uttermost parts of the earth in time measured in hours, not months. The Gospel can be preached in real time simultaneously to the entire earth by our Lord's living prophets. Those sent to Earth during the years leading up to the Restoration, and since the Restoration, have been saved to come to Earth and prepare everything needful for our Lord's return. The Lord's hand is in all things as He has made clear in a revelation to Joseph Smith in the same year of 1831:

Doctrine and Covenants Section 59:

21 And in nothing doth man offend God, or against none is his wrath kindled, save those who confess not his hand in all things, and obey not his commandments.

Men and women who became great scientists and inventors, along with many others needed to apply what has been revealed, have been inspired by God to change our world to make it possible to preach the Gospel to everyone.

It is true that Lucifer has used knowledge gained via divine revelation to hinder the work of God. But Satan cannot succeed in his efforts to stop the work of the Restoration in preparation for our Lord's return. John Wentworth, who was editor of the newspaper *The Chicago Democrat* in the years immediately before the Prophet Joseph Smith was killed by a mob in Carthage, Illinois, wrote to Joseph and asked him to write a history of The Church of Jesus Christ of Latter-day Saints. Joseph's response, known as the *Wentworth Letter*, concludes with a magnificent statement about the destiny of our Lord's Restored Gospel. After that statement, the Prophet included a summary of the beliefs of the new church. That summary is known today as "The Articles of Faith," and is included in my Quad just after the Pearl of Great Price. Here are the statement and the summary of beliefs at the concluding part of the *Wentworth Letter*, published in the March 1, 1842, edition of the *Times and Seasons*, a newspaper of The Church of Jesus Christ of Latter-day Saints in Nauvoo, Illinois:

> *Our missionaries are going forth to different nations, and in Germany, Palestine, New Holland, Australia, the East Indies, and other places, the Standard of Truth has been erected; no unhallowed hand can stop the work from progressing; persecutions may rage, mobs may combine, armies may assemble, calumny may defame, but the truth of God will go forth boldly, nobly, and independent, till it has penetrated every continent, visited every clime, swept every country, and sounded in every ear; till the purposes of God shall be accomplished, and the Great Jehovah shall say the work is done.*

> *[The Articles of Faith]*
>
> *We believe in God, the Eternal Father, and in His Son, Jesus Christ, and in the Holy Ghost.*

We believe that men will be punished for their own sins, and not for Adam's transgression.

We believe that through the Atonement of Christ, all mankind may be saved, by obedience to the laws and ordinances of the Gospel.

We believe that the first principles and ordinances of the Gospel are: first, Faith in the Lord Jesus Christ; second, Repentance; third, Baptism by immersion for the remission of sins; fourth, Laying on [of] hands for the gift of the Holy Ghost.

We believe that a man must be called of God, by prophecy, and by the laying on hands by those who are in authority, to preach the Gospel and administer in the ordinances thereof.

We believe in the same organization that existed in the Primitive Church, namely, apostles, prophets, pastors, teachers, evangelists, and so forth.

We believe in the gift of tongues, prophecy, revelation, visions, healing, interpretation of tongues, and so forth.

We believe the Bible to be the word of God as far as it is translated correctly; we also believe the Book of Mormon to be the word of God.

We believe all that God has revealed, all that He does now reveal, and we believe that He will yet reveal many great and important things pertaining to the Kingdom of God.

We believe in the literal gathering of Israel and in the restoration of the Ten Tribes; that Zion (the New Jerusalem) will be built upon the American continent; that Christ will reign personally upon the earth; and, that the earth will be renewed and receive its paradisiacal glory.

We claim the privilege of worshiping Almighty God according to the dictates of our own conscience, and allow all men the same privilege, let them worship how, where, or what they may.

We believe in being subject to kings, presidents, rulers, and magistrates, in obeying, honoring, and sustaining the law.

We believe in being honest, true, chaste, benevolent, virtuous, and in doing good to all men; indeed, we may say that we follow the admonition of Paul—We believe all things, we hope all things, we have endured many things, and hope to be able to endure all things. If there is anything virtuous, lovely, or of good report or praiseworthy, we seek after these things.

Respectfully, etc.,
Joseph Smith

While working with the Interfaith Council of Metropolitan Washington (IFC), I had an interesting experience with the Articles of Faith. Not long after I joined the IFC Board, the Chair of one of the IFC committees asked me to review, and revise, if necessary, a summary of the doctrine of The Church of Jesus Christ of Latter-day Saints that was soon to be re-published and sent to schools around the United States. The IFC published in booklet form a brief statement of beliefs of its member faith groups and was getting ready to send out a revised edition. As I read the booklet that was being revised, I was impressed. Students reading the IFC publication could gain a good idea of the teachings of the major religions of the world. Of course, I was particularly interested in what was written about the beliefs of The Church of Jesus Christ of Latter-day Saints; and discovered that my predecessor had done a good job stating our beliefs and had followed the format of the other religions. I almost told the Committee Chair that our submission would not need to be revised but decided to sleep on the decision.

By the time of the IFC Board's next meeting when I needed to give the Chair a decision, I was convinced that the submission of The Church of Jesus Christ of Latter-day Saints did not need to be revised – it needed to be replaced. I submitted the Articles of Faith penned by the Prophet Joseph Smith in his letter to Editor John Wentworth in 1842 as the summary of beliefs of The Church of Jesus Christ of Latter-day Saints. What I did not expect was the push back that came almost immediately from some of the other faith leaders. There was such a contrast between the Articles of Faith and the submissions by other faiths that a few faith leaders were disturbed with the change. I explained to the Board that a living prophet of God had written our Articles of Faith, and I could not improve on what he had written. I then suggested that each faith leader should have the right to place his or her content in the booklet being sent out. Most of the Board members supported me and the change stood. That little incident was the beginning of lasting friendships that I have made with faith leaders on the Interfaith Council of Metropolitan Washington.

The Book of Mormon is an extraordinary book, written over a thousand years by prophets of God that lived in the Americas. It was then buried in the ground for over a thousand years to be brought forth in our day by a living prophet of God. It was to become the keystone of The Church of Jesus Christ of Latter-day Saints. It serves as proof that our Heavenly Father has commenced the work of preparing to send Jesus Christ back to Earth in great glory to reign for a thousand years. It has also been the means to prove by the Holy Spirit that Joseph Smith was a prophet of God, and that

The Church of Jesus Christ of Latter-day Saints is the Lord's true church restored in the last days before our Lord returns. Beginning with my investigation of the Restored Gospel, I have often reflected about prophesies given and prophetic actions taken by prophets on earth since the year 1830 when the Book of Mormon was published. Here are a few prophesies and actions of living prophets that have made an impression on me:

1. Section 87 of the Doctrine and Covenants is a revelation that was received by Joseph Smith on Christmas Day 1833 and published not long after it was received. In Section 87 the Lord reveals to his Prophet that there will be a civil war in the United States; and that the civil war will be a beginning of war between nations. The Northern States will be against the Southern States over the issue of slavery and the war will begin with the rebellion of South Carolina. This prophecy was given more than a quarter century before South Carolina fired on Fort Sumter on April 12, 1861:

    Doctrine and Covenants Section 87

    1 Verily, thus saith the Lord concerning the wars that will shortly come to pass, beginning at the rebellion of South Carolina, which will eventually terminate in the death and misery of many souls;

    2 And the time will come that war will be poured out upon all nations, beginning at this place.

3 For behold, the Southern States shall be divided against the Northern States, and the Southern States will call on other nations, even the nation of Great Britain, as it is called, and they shall also call upon other nations, in order to defend themselves against other nations; and then war shall be poured out upon all nations.

4 And it shall come to pass, after many days, slaves shall rise up against their masters, who shall be marshaled and disciplined for war.

5 And it shall come to pass also that the remnants who are left of the land will marshal themselves, and shall become exceedingly angry, and shall vex the Gentiles with a sore vexation.

6 And thus, with the sword and by bloodshed the inhabitants of the earth shall mourn; and with famine, and plague, and earthquake, and the thunder of heaven, and the fierce and vivid lightning also, shall the inhabitants of the earth be made to feel the wrath, and indignation, and chastening hand of an Almighty God, until the consumption decreed hath made a full end of all nations;

7 That the cry of the saints, and of the blood of the saints, shall cease to come up into the ears of the Lord of Sabaoth, from the earth, to be avenged of their enemies.

8 Wherefore, stand ye in holy places, and be not moved, until the day of the Lord come; for behold, it cometh quickly, saith the Lord. Amen

Beginning in 1861 with the civil war in the United States, war has been poured out upon nations on a scale never before imagined, and the prophecies in Section 87 are still being fulfilled.

2. As discussed in Chapter 3, the Prophet Joseph Smith called Apostle Orson Hyde to go to Palestine and dedicate the Holy Land for return of the Jews. Orson Hyde's dedicatory prayer was given on the Mount of Olives in 1841 and published to the world at that time. Shortly after Orson Hyde's prayer of dedication, Joseph Smith included in the Wentworth Letter published in March 1842 the Articles of Faith of The Church of Jesus Christ of Latter-day Saints. Article of Faith 10 includes our belief in the literal gathering of Israel. In 1948, 106 years after his letter to John Wentworth was published, and 107 years after Orson Hyde's dedicatory prayer, Israel was established as a nation in the Holy Land. When the United Nations voted to approve the State of Israel as a member nation and homeland for the Jewish people, David Ben-Gurion, who was leader of the World Zionist Organization, said that modern Israel was the first Jewish state in 2000 years. However, two thousand years ago, at the time of the mortal ministry of our Savior, Israel was under Roman rule. It had actually been closer to three millennia since there was a sovereign Jewish nation.

3. Section 89 of the Doctrine and Covenants
   Section 89 is discussed in Chapter 10, dealing with the necessity of sacrifice. However, we know that obeying the Word of Wisdom is not a sacrifice. Michio Kushi was certainly impressed that in 1833 the Prophet Joseph Smith knew the same principles of nutrition that Michio was teaching in the regimen he called macrobiotics.

4. Family Home Evening

    On April 27, 1915, the living prophet, President of The Church of Jesus Christ of Latter-day Saints, Joseph F. Smith, recommended that members hold a family home evening each week. Brigham Young before him, and other living prophets in our time, have also advised holding a family home evening. Here is part of President Joseph F. Smith's letter:

Letter from Joseph F. Smith, President of The Church of Jesus Christ of Latter-day Saints, April 27, 1915:

We advise and urge the inauguration of a 'Home Evening' throughout the church, at which time fathers and mothers may gather their boys and girls about them in the home and teach them the word of the Lord. ...

This 'Home Evening' should be devoted to prayer, singing hymns, songs, instrumental music, scripture-reading, family topics and specific instruction on the principles of the gospel, and on the ethical problems of life, as well as the duties and obligations of children to parents, the home, the Church, society and the nation. For the smaller children appropriate recitations, songs, stories and games may be introduced. Light refreshments of such a nature as may be largely prepared in the home might be served.

If the Saints obey this counsel, we promise that great blessings will result. Love at home and obedience to parents will increase. Faith will be developed in the hearts of the youth of Israel, and they will gain power to combat the evil influence and temptations which beset them.

When missionaries, Elders Buhler and Hoopes, taught Sharon and me about family home evenings, we knew immediately that holding family home evenings would be a good thing for our family. We had two 4-year-old daughters, and we wanted our home to be like the home described by President Joseph F. Smith in his 1915 letter. In the years after 1915, Family Home Evening was standardized throughout The Church of Jesus Christ of Latter-day Saints to be Monday nights. No other meetings were to be scheduled on Monday nights, so that members could count on having the time available to be with their families. Although Sharon and I were both very involved in activities outside of the family, we knew that an evening dedicated solely to our family could pay big dividends, just like the Prophet said it would.

Accordingly, Sharon and I made a pact with each other that Monday nights were to be devoted to our family. By the time we were baptized in 1978, the Church had developed great manuals for families to use to plan and conduct family home evenings. We obtained a family home evening manual and used it faithfully. Soon our children knew that Monday nights were for family, and they looked forward to reporting on their week's activities and helping to organize and make our family home evenings successful learning experiences while at the same time having fun. For my part, unless I was in the middle of a trial, I considered Monday nights sacred time and refused to let any matter outside the home interfere with family home evenings.

One of my activities outside the family was supporting the Red Cross. I was serving on the local Red Cross Board of Directors and attended meetings and activities faithfully. It was inevitable that the time would come when I would have a conflict with family home evening and my responsibility to some other group or cause. That conflict came with the Fairfax County, Virginia, Chapter of the American Red Cross. The Chairman at the time was the CEO of a large company who gave of his time unselfishly. He was a really nice fellow, and I liked him a lot. In an effort to raise money, some Red Cross Board members wanted the Red Cross to start sponsoring Bingo games. I was familiar with the issue, and the Chairman knew that I was up to speed because of my prior service as a member of the Virginia Legislature. The Chairman called a special meeting of the Board and scheduled the meeting for a Monday night.

Right after calling the meeting for Monday night, the Chairman of the Board called me and said: "Jim, I know that Monday night is your family night, but this is an important meeting. By my count the Board is evenly divided, and I need you there to make sure this gambling motion does not pass. The Red Cross should not be promoting gambling." I agreed with the Chairman about the Bingo issue, but told him that if he wanted me there, he would have to schedule the meeting on a night other than Monday night. He replied that there was no other night. "Be there," he said and hung up the phone.

Monday evening came and I did not attend the special Red Cross Board meeting. The Bingo vote resulted in a tie and the meeting had to be re-scheduled. This time the Chair picked a night other than Monday night and the Bingo motion ultimately failed. However, my relationship with the Chairman soured and not long after that I left the Red Cross Board. A few years passed, and you can imagine my surprise when the former Red Cross Chairman made an appointment to see me about a case. He had been seriously injured in an accident because of the negligence of a local merchant and wanted me to represent him. I was very surprised that he would ask me to be his lawyer and told him so.

He said: "Jim, I came to you because of your firm resolve and practice of family home evening as advocated by The Church of Jesus Christ of Latter-day Saints. It is my way of saying 'thank you' for showing me the way to care for my own family." I was certainly intrigued by his response and asked him to tell me more. The former Chairman said that he had a daughter who became very rebellious when she reached the age of 16. Neither he nor his wife could handle her, and it became so bad that he was afraid she would be lost to his family. He remembered our dispute over the Bingo meeting time while we were serving together on the Fairfax Red Cross Board. The former Chairman did not change his religious affiliation, but he did get a family home evening manual from a friend who was a member of The Church of Jesus Christ of Latter-day Saints. He began to hold weekly family home evenings using the manual as a template. He reported that everything about his family was now much better, and his daughter was doing great.

5. Family Preparedness
    In the Priesthood Session of the General Conference of The Church of Jesus Christ of Latter-day Saints on

October 5, 1996, the then living Prophet of the Lord, Gordon B. Hinckley, reported on his interview with Mike Wallace of the CBS 60 Minutes program. In that interview President Hinckley was asked about family preparedness. Here is Mr. Wallace's question, and President Hinckley's answer:

Question: "Why are members of the Church expected to keep a year's supply of food, clothing, and fuel?"

Reply: "We teach self-reliance as a principle of life, that we ought to provide for ourselves and take care of our own needs. And so we encourage our people to have something, to plan ahead, keep ... food on hand, to establish a savings account, if possible, against a rainy day. Catastrophes come to people sometimes when least expected—unemployment, sickness, things of that kind. The individual, as we teach, ought to do for himself all that he can. When he has exhausted his resources, he ought to turn to his family to assist him. When the family can't do it, the Church takes over. And when the Church takes over, our great desire is to first take care of his immediate needs and then to help him for so long as he needs to be helped, but in that process to assist him in training, in securing employment, in finding some way of getting on his feet again. That's the whole objective of this great welfare program."

It took me ten years and 3 sets of missionaries to finally read the Book of Mormon as the Prophet Moroni directs. About five years into that ten-year span, my law partner and his wife invited Sharon and me out to dinner to see their new home. Doug and Ginny Bywater had designed and supervised the construction of their home and we were totally impressed. In fact, two or three years later we bought a lot to build a new home and Sharon patterned our home after the one Doug and Ginny designed. After dinner, as we finished our tour of the Bywater's new home and went down to see the then unfinished basement, I looked over at one wall and saw a lot of shelves. As I looked closer I saw a tremendous amount of food on those basement shelves. I said: "Doug, what in the world is that?" He answered: "That is our year's supply of food. Our church teaches us that we should be prepared to take care of our families in case disaster strikes." On the way home after our dinner and tour with the Bywater's, I said to Sharon: "Sharon, we need to change churches. The Bywater's church has got it together much better than our church." I will not soon forget her reply: "Tate, you will stay in our church. You just need to become more active." Five years later, when we finally became members of The Church of Jesus Christ of Latter-day Saints, one of the first things I did was build shelves in our new home, patterned after the Bywater home, and acquire our year's supply. We are still eating some of the wheat I bought decades ago; and it is still good, nutritious food. The main point is that a good feeling inside comes from being prepared for disaster or hardship.

6. Defending the Family
    This is a time of rapid change, not only in science and technology, but also in family life. Many of our Heavenly Father's children have decided that they are smarter than their Maker and can best decide the rules by which life is created and nurtured. Lucifer has stepped up his game

during these latter days before our Lord returns. Satan is going for the jugular vein of mortality - the sanctity of life and the definition of "marriage". Recognizing the coming danger, the Lord's living profit, Gordon B. Hinckley, and the Lord's living Apostles issued A Proclamation to the World, defining and defending the traditional family. This proclamation on the family was published over two decades ago and made clear the mind and will of the Lord on family structure and individual responsibilities within families. Here is the Proclamation on the Family, first published on September 23, 1995:

The Family: A Proclamation to the World

Gordon B. Hinckley President of the Church

We, the First Presidency and the Council of the Twelve Apostles of The Church of Jesus Christ of Latter-day Saints, solemnly proclaim that marriage between a man and a woman is ordained of God and that the family is central to the Creator's plan for the eternal destiny of His children.

All human beings—male and female—are created in the image of God. Each is a beloved spirit son or daughter of heavenly parents, and, as such, each has a divine nature and destiny.

Gender is an essential characteristic of individual premortal, mortal, and eternal identity and purpose.

In the premortal realm, spirit sons and daughters knew and worshiped God as their Eternal Father and accepted His plan by which His children could obtain a physical body and gain earthly experience to progress toward perfection and ultimately realize his or her divine destiny as an heir of eternal life.

The divine plan of happiness enables family relationships to be perpetuated beyond the grave. Sacred ordinances and covenants available in holy temples make it possible for individuals to return to the presence of God and for families to be united eternally.

The first commandment that God gave to Adam and Eve pertained to their potential for parenthood as husband and wife. We declare that God's commandment for His children to multiply and replenish the earth remains in force.

We further declare that God has commanded that the sacred powers of procreation are to be employed only between man and woman, lawfully wedded as husband and wife. We declare the means by which mortal life is created to be divinely appointed.

We affirm the sanctity of life and of its importance in God's eternal plan.

Husband and wife have a solemn responsibility to love and care for each other and for their children. "Children are an heritage of the Lord" (Psalms 127:3). Parents have a sacred duty to rear their children in love and righteousness, to provide for their physical and spiritual needs, to teach them to love and serve one another, to observe the commandments of God and to be law-abiding citizens wherever they live. Husbands and wives—mothers and fathers—will be held accountable before God for the discharge of these obligations.

The family is ordained of God. Marriage between man and woman is essential to His eternal plan. Children are entitled to birth within the bonds of matrimony, and to be reared by a father and a mother who honor marital vows with complete fidelity.

Happiness in family life is most likely to be achieved when founded upon the teachings of the Lord Jesus Christ. Successful marriages and families are established and maintained on principles of faith, prayer, repentance, forgiveness, *respect, love, compassion, work, and wholesome recreational activities.*

By divine design, fathers are to preside over their families in love and righteousness and are responsible to provide the necessities of life and protection for their families. Mothers are primarily responsible for the nurture of their children. In these sacred responsibilities, fathers and mothers are obligated to help one another as equal partners.

Disability, death, or other circumstances may necessitate individual adaptation. Extended families should lend support when needed.

We warn that individuals who violate covenants of chastity, who abuse spouse or offspring, or who fail to fulfill family responsibilities will one day stand accountable before God.

Further, we warn that the disintegration of the family will bring upon individuals, communities, and nations the calamities foretold by ancient and modern prophets.

We call upon responsible citizens and officers of government everywhere to promote those measures designed to maintain and strengthen the family as the fundamental unit of society.

This proclamation was read by President Gordon B. Hinckley as part of his message at the General Relief Society Meeting held September 23, 1995, in Salt Lake City, Utah.

Thirteen years after publication of the Proclamation on the Family by The Church of Jesus Christ of Latter-day Saints, while I was serving as President of the Alabama Birmingham Mission, I received an email from Don Wildmon, who was the leader and founder of the American Family Association, a large organization headquartered in Tupelo, Mississippi, that supported traditional marriage. He wanted to thank our then living prophet, President Thomas S. Monson, for the Church's support of Proposition 8 in California that had just passed. Petitions were included with his message, and he wanted me to make sure that the petitions reached President Monson.

Shortly after I received the "thank you" message from the pro family organization, I also received a call from a dear friend who was serving as President of the California Los Angeles Mission. President Spencer (Tim) Blackburn and his wife, Jan, were delayed as they tried to return to the mission home - located on the grounds of the Los Angeles Temple of The Church of Jesus Christ of Latter-day Saints - on election night in 2008 when Proposition 8 passed in California. The Los Angeles Temple was surrounded by riot police holding back a hostile mob that was angry about Church support for Proposition 8. Supporters of traditional marriage in California had prevailed at the ballot box; but it was clear that those seeking change in the fundamental rules governing family life were a long way from throwing in the towel and were willing to engage in violent protests to advance their cause.

As President Blackburn and I talked about the election campaign in California and the Church's participation in that campaign, he shared the experience of a young Stake President in Southern California who was asked to come to an interfaith meeting of churches supporting Proposition 8. In The Church of Jesus Christ of Latter-day Saints, we do not have paid clergy. Stake

Presidents, who preside over a number of congregations (Wards or Branches), are called by inspiration by General Authorities of the Church. In this particular case, the Stake President was newly called to preside over the members in his Stake when he received the invitation to attend the interfaith meeting.

For some reason as he walked out of his home to attend the interfaith meeting, the Stake President put a copy of the Proclamation on the Family in his coat pocket. Shortly after the meeting began, the person conducting the meeting called on the newly called Stake President to come forward and explain why The Church of Jesus Christ of Latter-day Saints was supporting Proposition 8. When he reached the podium, the Stake President reached in his pocket and pulled out the Proclamation on the Family and read it to the assembled group. After he finished reading the Family Proclamation, there was silence for a time, then everyone stood and gave the new Stake President a standing ovation.

This experience that the new Stake President had with the interfaith group is a vivid illustration of the power of the Word of the Lord when it reaches receptive ears. The Proclamation on the Family is the mind of the Lord and the will of the Lord as proclaimed by his living Prophet in our time. We will do well to listen to our Lord's Prophets and obey them.

Chapter Twelve

Personal Revelation

Experience is an important part of learning to recognize revelation from God. The more we act on divine revelation, the more revelation we will receive. Obedience to revelation will also make it easier and easier for us to discern thoughts coming from God, thoughts originating with us, and thoughts coming from Satan.

Personal revelation is given to all of God's children. It is our responsibility as children of God to take the steps necessary to know when we are receiving personal revelation.

I am convinced that our Heavenly Father sends personal revelation to all of his children – not just church leaders. The challenge is to know when revelation is coming from God and when it is coming from somewhere else. We may, and often do, receive revelation to do something hard, but we will never, ever, receive revelation from God asking us to do something evil. Conversely, we will never receive revelation from Satan encouraging us to do something good. If we study the Word of God as found in ancient and modern scriptures, and if we obey our Lord's commandments, we will have the tools we need to discern not only between truth and error, but to decide if the thoughts and impressions we are receiving are coming from the Holy Ghost. The other ingredient necessary to discern revelation is experience. The more we act on divine revelation, the more revelation we will receive. Obedience to revelation will also make it easier and easier for us to discern thoughts coming from God, thoughts originating with us, and thoughts coming from Satan.

A knowledge of truth is something all of God's children are entitled to if we will ask for it. In fact, if we have a testimony of Jesus Christ, remember Him in all that we do, and obey His commandments, we will have His Spirit to be with us as taught in the sacrament prayers of The Church of Jesus Christ of Latter-day Saints. And, if we have a testimony of Jesus and His Spirit with us, we will have the Spirit of Prophecy – a lesson taught to John the Revelator by an angel of the Lord as recorded in the Book of Revelation in the New Testament of the Bible. Here are the sacrament prayers and the scripture declaring that a testimony of Jesus is the spirit of prophecy. Note that the sacrament prayers reproduced in Chapter 7, that were taken from the Book of Mormon, are identical to the prayers given to the Prophet Joseph Smith in Section 20 of the Doctrine and Covenants. Water has now been substituted for wine in the second prayer:

The Sacrament Prayer to Bless the Bread:
Doctrine and Covenants Section 20:

77 O God, the Eternal Father, we ask thee in the name of thy Son, Jesus Christ, to bless and sanctify this bread to the souls of all those who partake of it, that they may eat in remembrance of the body of thy Son, and witness unto thee, O God, the Eternal Father, that they are willing to take upon them the name of thy Son, and always remember him and keep his commandments which he has given them; that they may always have his Spirit to be with them. Amen.

The Sacrament Prayer to Bless the Water:

Doctrine and Covenants Section 20:

79 O God, the Eternal Father, we ask thee in the name of thy Son, Jesus Christ, to bless and sanctify this wine to the souls of all those who drink of it, that they may do it in remembrance of the blood of thy Son, which was shed for them; that they may witness unto thee, O God, the Eternal Father, that they do always remember him, that they may have his Spirit to be with them. Amen.

A Testimony of Jesus Christ is the Spirit of Prophecy:

Revelations Chapter 19:

10 And I fell at his feet to worship him. And he said unto me, See thou do it not: I am thy fellowservant, and of thy brethren that have the testimony of Jesus: worship God: for the testimony of Jesus is the spirit of prophecy.

The Kingdom of God is a kingdom of order. Revelation from Heaven comes to those who need it. For example, parents receive revelation on how to manage their homes and rear their children. Children and adults receive revelation on how they should live their lives and about upcoming events in their lives. Bishops and other church leaders receive revelation about how to lead their congregations, and about which members should be called to serve in the various organizations of the Church. The President of The Church of Jesus Christ of Latter-day Saints receives revelation for the whole Church; and revelation for the benefit of all people living on the Earth. Civic leaders who sincerely seek Divine help will receive revelation on how to guide and lead communities and nations.

Not many weeks after my baptism in 1978 I was called to work with the youth and attended an area wide youth conference. At the conclusion of the conference, which I later learned was a tradition practiced at most youth conferences, a testimony meeting was held. Youth would get up and speak as moved upon by the Spirit and share their testimony of Jesus. There were several black youths at this conference, even though the right for African Americans to hold the Priesthood had only been restored a few weeks prior to the conference. One black youth, aged 16 or 17, got up to share his testimony of the Restoration of the Gospel.

This black youth came from a very large family. There were twelve children and the whole family attended their protestant church services faithfully every Sunday morning. He related that his family sat on the front two rows of his chapel, and he usually sat right in front of the preacher. One Sunday morning earlier that year as church service was in progress, he looked up at the preacher and the ceiling above the preacher and was astonished at what he saw. The whole top of the Church building came off and an angel came right down from Heaven and stood above the preacher. He could no longer hear the preacher but could hear what the angel was saying with perfect clarity. The angel said to him that he would hold the Priesthood and would go out into the world to preach the Gospel of Jesus Christ. The vision then closed.

Within a week of his vision, this young black man was walking along a street in his hometown and two missionaries of The Church of Jesus Christ of Latter-day Saints came up to him. Somehow he knew that the vision he had seen and these two young men were related. He listened to the message the missionaries had for him, began the lessons, and soon was baptized a member of The Church of Jesus Christ of Latter-day Saints. I kept up with the young man and learned that a few years later he was called on a two-year mission to Africa and was able to become a part of the great work of opening that continent to the Restored Gospel.

In September 2006 I was called to be a Mission President of The Church of Jesus Christ of Latter-day Saints to serve for three years, beginning in July 2007. President Boyd K. Packer, who presided over the Quorum of Twelve Apostles at the time, met with us together in his hotel room at the Dulles Airport Marriott and gave us the assignment. Sharon asked President Packer if he knew where we would be called to serve. President Packer replied that he only knew where we would not be called. They had recently called a Mission President that had a very large family, and the mission home in St. Louis was the only home in the worldwide church big enough to house his family. President Packer then said that Church practice was to send out notices of particular mission assignments around the first of March.

About a month before March 1, 2007, about 3 a.m., I had a vivid dream in which my legal secretary gave me a letter and said: "You will be going to Birmingham, Alabama."

I immediately got up with a strong feeling that this dream was revelation from the Lord. I did not tell Sharon, but instead immediately wrote a letter to my secretary, sealed it, and carried it to work the next day. I asked my partner, Doug Bywater, and the secretary to come into my office and gave the secretary the letter. As I handed her the letter, I told her about my dream and said that I would know if the letter contained revelation in about a month.

Just as President Packer predicted, a month later the letter came to our home. I was not home; and despite Sharon's impatience to learn where we would be living for the next three years, she waited until she could get me on the phone before opening the letter. As soon as I saw that she was calling, I knew she had received the letter, that my dream would be confirmed, and that we would be living in Alabama for the next three years.

The revelation about our assignment to the Alabama Birmingham Mission confirmed to me that Sharon and I were called by God to that assignment. I had another experience with personal revelation which is very sacred to me that I will share. Sharon and I are the only members of The Church of Jesus Christ of Latter-day Saints in our respective families. We come from great families, and I am afraid that we have not been as effective missionaries to them as we should have been. The Lord has provided a way, however, for his sons and daughters to receive essential Gospel ordinances vicariously in holy Temples after their death. Our mortal bodies return to earth, but our spirits were neither created nor destroyed on Earth. In other words, we don't die – we are just transferred to another place. People who have departed mortality can still accept the Gospel of Jesus Christ in the next world and benefit from Gospel ordinances such as baptism.

The Lord's Temples, and the work done in those Temples for those who have departed mortality, provide an answer to those who deny that God exists; or say that they have no intention of following a God who would send people to hell who had no chance to become a Christian. As of December 31, 2021, as reported at the April 2022 General Conference of The Church of Jesus Christ of Latter-day Saints, there were 170 Temples in operation around the World. It is my belief that there will be well over 1000 Temples operating all over the World before the Lord returns. Everyone will have the opportunity to accept or reject the Gospel - either in this life or in the spirit world that follows this life -because our Heavenly Father is just. The Apostle Paul was trying to explain the principle of eternal life and the coming resurrection to settle a doctrinal dispute between the Pharisees and Sadducees. The Sadducees did not believe in the resurrection; but Paul reasoned with them – why do we do vicarious baptisms for the dead if there is no resurrection? The scripture is found in First Corinthians, Chapter 15, verse 29. Verses 12 – 29 are included in **NOTE 19** in the Appendix (Page 248) to put Paul's argument in context..

First Corinthians 15:29

29 Else what shall they do which are baptized for the dead, if the dead rise not at all? why are they then baptized for the dead?

In addition to baptisms and other ordinances for the dead, ordinances sealing families together for all eternity, not just until death, are performed in the temples of The Church of Jesus Christ of Latter-day Saints. My Dad died in the summer of 2008 while Sharon and I were serving in the Alabama Birmingham Mission. It is Church policy that one year after death, Temple ordinances can be performed for the dead. I was anxious to have the sealing ordinances performed, so as soon as the year was up, in the summer of 2009, Sharon and I went to the Birmingham Alabama Temple to act as proxies for my father and mother.

The Temple Sealer was J. Reid Giles, who was a former President of the Birmingham Alabama Temple. Upon his release as Temple President, I called him as a counselor in the Alabama Birmingham Mission Presidency. During the sealing ceremony, there are two witnesses, one witness on each side of the sealer, whose purpose is to make sure the sealing ordinance is correctly performed. As Sharon and I kneeled across the alter acting as proxy for my parents' eternal marriage, I looked up at President Giles and the two men next to him and I had an immediate revelation. I knew that they were men of God, that the ordinance was real, and that my parents would joyfully accept the sealing ordinance.

Then the Lord did something for me that he did not need to do – he gave me a revelation and prophecy that did not directly concern me but did affirm that prophecy and revelation are real. As I looked at one of the witnesses, Gary Pettus, I instantly knew that he would be called as the next President of the Tupelo Mississippi Stake at a Stake Conference to be held in a few weeks. What I did not know was that my good friend,

Elder Bruce Carlson of the Seventy, a General Authority of the Church, would receive the assignment to come to Tupelo and choose the new Stake President of the Tupelo Mississippi Stake.

When the time came for the Tupelo Stake Conference, Sharon and I drove from Birmingham to Tupelo the night before the Sunday Session of Stake Conference. By that time Bruce had been in touch. I knew he would be conducting meetings and interviews all day on Saturday to consider potential Stake Presidents and train Stake leaders; so, we agreed to meet for breakfast on Sunday morning. At that breakfast I told Bruce that the Lord had revealed to me who the new Stake President was going to be, so he did not need to tell me. Bruce Carlson is a man of great faith, and when I made that statement, he did not reply, nor did we discuss the matter further. On Sunday morning, Gary Pettus was called and sustained by the members as the new Tupelo Stake President. Like Sharon and me, President Pettus was contacted by the missionaries in mid-life, long after he left his boyhood home, received a testimony from the Holy Spirit that the Book of Mormon was the word of God, and was baptized a member of The Church of Jesus Christ of Latter-day Saints.

Time passed and Elder Bruce Carlson received Emeritus Status as a General Authority of the Church. Sharon and I returned from our mission in Alabama and resumed what had been a normal life for us. Part of that life is sailing. We are blue water sailors and like to sail from our home on the Chesapeake Bay to New England for summer holiday. Several years ago, a few years before the pandemic, my daughter, Virginia Isaacson, and her husband, Tom Isaacson - who are also sailors - invited us for a sail with friends on our jointly owned sloop. Sharon and I are now seasoned citizens, and most of our sailing is with Ginny and Tom and crew recruited by them. During this particular day-sail on the Patuxent River, we met Tom and Ginny's friends – a delightful couple who were also sailors. The husband, Doug, was retired military and was working as a Government contractor in the Washington, D.C. area.

As I got to know Doug, I learned that he had been on Bruce Carlson's staff when Bruce was Commanding General of Eighth Air Force. As soon as I had the opportunity, I contacted Bruce and told him about Doug. I knew that Bruce also loved to sail; so I suggested that during the next blue water sailing opportunity it would be great if Doug and Bruce could join us on an ocean leg of our trip as part of the crew. After getting to know Doug and his family, I felt that the Lord wanted them to become members of The Church of Jesus Christ of Latter-day Saints and carry part of the load of building our Lord's Kingdom on Earth.

Bruce and Doug both agreed to join us on the ocean leg of our return from New England that next summer. Our usual crew is about 8 able bodied sailors, which gives us four 2 person watches to cover the 24 hours in a day. I assigned Bruce and Doug as watch mates so that they would have plenty of opportunity to re-live old times. There is nothing quite like sailing on the open ocean in the middle of the night when the weather is good – as it was on this trip – for encouraging deep thought about things that really matter in life.

As it turned out, we were at sea on a Sunday, and we followed our custom of having a Church service on board.

For this particular service, we decided to have a testimony meeting and share our thoughts about our Savior. At these testimony meetings aboard ship, there is no requirement that everyone share their thoughts. However, what usually happens is that everyone aboard loves the Lord and is eager to share with others their love for our Savior. We all gather in the cockpit for the service, have a prayer (and sometimes a song if singers are present) and then take turns sharing our testimonies in order of seating.

When it came my turn, I suddenly remembered my revelation about Gary Pettus being chosen as the Tupelo Stake President. I asked Bruce: "Do you know how I know that Gary Pettus was chosen by God to be the Tupelo Stake President, and that you had the Spirit of the Lord with you when you chose him?" I was not sure that Bruce would even remember choosing Gary, because I knew that he had presided at a lot of stake conferences. Bruce remembered, and I told him about the revelation I had in the Birmingham Alabama Temple weeks before the Tupelo Mississippi Stake Conference. To my surprise, Bruce was not surprised that the Lord had revealed to me that Gary Pettus was to be the new Stake President. Then Bruce taught me a lesson. He said: "The Lord chooses His leaders. It was my job to go to Tupelo and discover whom the Lord had picked to be the new Stake President."

Personal revelation is given to all of God's children. It is our responsibility as children of God to take the steps necessary to know when we are receiving personal revelation. If we are obeying our Lord's commandments, and always remember Him, we will have the Spirit of the Lord with us. The promise is sure because the Lord does not lie. The Spirit of the Lord will guide us to discern divine revelation, accept divine revelation, and reject revelation that comes from Satan. When divine revelation comes to us, it is our duty to obey – no matter how difficult obedience may be. The Lord will not give us revelation if he has not prepared the way for us to follow His instructions.

Nephi, the ancient American prophet, faced a difficult assignment from the Lord when obeying a revelation from God that was received by his father, Lehi. As recorded in the Book of Mormon, Nephi stated the principle this way:

Book of Mormon, 1 Nephi Chapter 3

*7 And it came to pass that I, Nephi, said unto my father: I will go and do the things which the Lord hath commanded, **for I know that the Lord giveth no commandments unto the children of men, save he shall prepare a way for them that they may accomplish the thing which he commandeth them.***

Nephi's revelation came to his father, but the Holy Spirit confirmed to Nephi that the revelation came from God. By this same principle of personal revelation, the Holy Spirit will reveal to us the truth of all things if we have faith in our Lord Jesus Christ, repent of our sins, and obey His commandments.

Chapter Thirteen

The Commandments are Not a Cafeteria

*Earth is a classroom for our Heavenly Father's children. It is our duty to become like Him and our Savior, Jesus Christ. To become perfect, we must do the very best we can to obey **all** of God's commandments.*

Many have the idea that it is up to us to decide which of our Lord's commandments to obey. If we want to indulge our lust, we forget about the commandment not to commit adultery. If we want to satisfy our greed, we fail to remember the commandment not to steal. We think that the commandments given to guide us through life are like entrees in a café – we go through the line, pick out the ones we like and ignore the rest. If we want to reach our potential and tap into the eternal world that we cannot see, but is real, we must do our best to obey all commandments – and repent as fast as we can when we fall short. Those who commit adultery will forfeit the joy of a happy family. Those who steal fail to give value in return for what they receive. Even if they are successful in avoiding sanctions imposed by man's law, thieves will never be truly happy or learn the lessons of mortality. Those who fail to honor their parents not only violate the Lord's commandment but make themselves unworthy to benefit from a commandment with promise.

Beginning with Adam and Eve, our Heavenly Father has given commandments, which if obeyed, will help us reach our potential as sons and daughters of God. In the Old Testament, we have a record of an important dispensation as Moses was called to lead the people of Israel out of slavery in Egypt. As he led the covenant people into the wilderness, Moses was commanded to meet with the Lord and receive what we refer to as the Ten Commandments – a textbook from God on how to behave in mortality. Here are the commandments as recorded in the second of the five books of Moses found in the Old Testament – Exodus:

Exodus Chapter 20

1 And God spake all these words, saying,

2 I am the Lord thy God, which have brought thee out of the land of Egypt, out of the house of bondage.

3 Thou shalt have no other gods before me. **_FIRST COMMANDMENT_**

4 Thou shalt not make unto thee any graven image, or any likeness of any thing that is in heaven above, or that is in the earth beneath, or that is in the water under the earth:

5 Thou shalt not bow down thyself to them, nor serve them: for I the Lord thy God am a jealous God, visiting the iniquity of the fathers upon the children unto the third and fourth generation of them that hate me;

6 And shewing mercy unto thousands of them that love me, and keep my commandments. **SECOND COMMANDMENT**

7 Thou shalt not take the name of the Lord thy God in vain; for the Lord will not hold him guiltless that taketh his name in vain. **THIRD COMMANDMENT**

8 Remember the sabbath day, to keep it holy.

9 Six days shalt thou labour, and do all thy work:

10 But the seventh day is the sabbath of the Lord thy God: in it thou shalt not do any work, thou, nor thy son, nor thy daughter, thy manservant, nor thy maidservant, nor thy cattle, nor thy stranger that is within thy gates:

11 For in six days the Lord made heaven and earth, the sea, and all that in them is, and rested the seventh day: wherefore the Lord blessed the sabbath day, and hallowed it. **FOURTH COMMANDMENT**

12 ¶ Honour thy father and thy mother: that thy days may be long upon the land which the Lord thy God giveth thee. **FIFTH COMMANDMENT**

13 Thou shalt not kill. **SIXTH COMMANDMENT**

14 Thou shalt not commit adultery. **SEVENTH COMMANDMENT**

15 Thou shalt not steal. **EIGHTH COMMANDMENT**

16 Thou shalt not bear false witness against thy neighbour. **NINTH COMMANDMENT**

17 Thou shalt not covet thy neighbour's house, thou shalt not covet thy neighbour's wife, nor his manservant, nor his maidservant, nor his ox, nor his ass, nor any thing that is thy neighbour's. **TENTH COMMANDMENT**

When the Lord came in the flesh, he gave two commandments that were intended to teach us a higher law and help us to understand the reasoning behind all commandments. Here are two commandments from the New Testament that form the basis of all the law:

Matthew Chapter 22

35 Then one of them, which was a lawyer, asked him a question, tempting him, and saying, 36 Master, which is the great commandment in the law?

*37 Jesus said unto him, **Thou shalt love the Lord thy God with all thy heart, and with all thy soul, and with all thy mind.** 38 This is the first and great commandment. **FIRST GREAT COMMANDMENT**￼*

*39 And the second is like unto it, **Thou shalt love thy neighbour as thyself. SECOND GREAT COMMANDMENT**￼*

40 On these two commandments hang all the law and the prophets.

The Book of Mormon gives us a record of our Lord's visit to the Americans shortly after His resurrection. One of the first things that the Lord did after our Heavenly Father introduced Jesus Christ to the multitude was to instruct those Americans to stop disputes between themselves and stop disputes about Christian doctrine. Jesus explained that Satan is in the middle of all disputes. The Savior then gave those people living in the Americas the higher law that He gave those living in Palestine as recorded in the New Testament of the Bible. The scripture given by the Lord himself to people living in the

New World about 34 A.D. recorded in 3ʳᵈ Nephi Chapter 11 is reproduced in **NOTE 20** in the Appendix (Page 249).

From Chapter 11 in 3rd Nephi in the Book of Mormon, once again we see the Lord prove the falsity of claims that the Jesus Christ of the Book of Mormon is different from the Jesus Christ of the Bible. In the Americas the Lord had the entire multitude feel the nail prints in His hands and in His feet and the wound in His side.

During His visit to the Americas after his resurrection, Jesus gave the ancient Americans instruction on how to live a good life, and the blessings that will flow from living such a life, much like those given to the Jews in what we call the Sermon on the Mount as recorded in the New Testament. The Lord's instructions are recorded in 3rd Nephi in the Book of Mormon, Chapter 12, which is reproduced in **NOTE 21** in the Appendix (Page 253).

When we fall short of perfect obedience to our Heavenly Father's commandments, we must speedily repent and do our best to be perfectly obedient. As time passes, and this process is repeated each day, we approach perfection. If we do our very best, that will be perfection for us; and the Lord will make up the difference through His atonement. Obedience is measured by choices we make every day between good and evil. The sum of those choices determines who we are. It is not what we do that really counts in the end – it is what we become that matters. We are children of God, and He wants us to become like Him. We don't want to be like Esau and sell our divine birthright for a bowl of soup.

About 550 B.C. the Prophet Nephi summarized Christ's commandments this way as recorded in the Book of Mormon:

Book of Mormon, 2 Nephi 26: 32

32 And again, the Lord God hath commanded that men should not murder; that they should not lie; that they should not steal; that they should not take the name of the Lord their God in vain; that they should not envy; that they should not have malice; that they should not contend one with another; that they should not commit whoredoms; and that they should do none of these things; for whoso doeth them shall perish.

In verses 23 – 33 of the same chapter Nephi explains that all commandments are given for the benefit of man. The Lord invites all to come unto Him and partake of His goodness – black, white, bond, free, male, female, heathen, Jew and Gentile. The Lord invites – it is our duty to come. Here is the scripture:

Book of Mormon, 2 Nephi 26:

23 For behold, my beloved brethren, I say unto you that the Lord God worketh not in darkness.

24 He doeth not anything save it be for the benefit of the world; for he loveth the world, even that he layeth down his own life that he may draw all men unto him. Wherefore, he commandeth none that they shall not partake of his salvation.

25 Behold, doth he cry unto any, saying: Depart from me? Behold, I say unto you, Nay; but he saith: Come unto me all ye ends of the earth, buy milk and honey, without money and without price.

26 Behold, hath he commanded any that they should depart out of the synagogues, or out of the houses of worship? Behold, I say unto you, Nay.

27 Hath he commanded any that they should not partake of his salvation? Behold I say unto you, Nay; but he hath given it free for all men; and he hath commanded his people that they should persuade all men to repentance.

28 Behold, hath the Lord commanded any that they should not partake of his goodness? Behold I say unto you, Nay; but all men are privileged the one like unto the other, and none are forbidden.

29 He commandeth that there shall be no priestcrafts; for, behold, priestcrafts are that men preach and set themselves up for a light unto the world, that they may get gain and praise of the world; but they seek not the welfare of Zion.

30 Behold, the Lord hath forbidden this thing; wherefore, the Lord God hath given a commandment that all men should have charity, which charity is love. And except they should have charity they were nothing. Wherefore, if they should have charity they would not suffer the laborer in Zion to perish.

31 But the laborer in Zion shall labor for Zion; for if they labor for money they shall perish.

32 And again, the Lord God hath commanded that men should not murder; that they should not lie; that they should not steal; that they should not take the name of the Lord their God in vain; that they should not envy; that they should not have malice; that they should not contend one with another; that they should not commit whoredoms; and that they should do none of these things; for whoso doeth them shall perish.

33 For none of these iniquities come of the Lord; for he doeth that which is good among the children of men; and he doeth

nothing save it be plain unto the children of men; and he inviteth them all to come unto him and partake of his goodness; and he denieth none that come unto him, black and white, bond and free, male and female; and he remembereth the heathen; and all are alike unto God, both Jew and Gentile.

Chapter Fourteen

The Book Of Mormon –
Third Nephi 29 , Third Nephi 30
A Message To Us

The Book of Mormon is the best kind of proof to convince the honest in heart that God lives, that Jesus is the Christ, and that our Heavenly Father has begun the work of sending His Son back in great glory to rule and reign on the Earth.

Just to make sure that he has left no doubt of our duty, in the final Chapters of 3rd Nephi the Lord has instructed His Prophet to spell out what is expected of those who are not yet numbered with the House of Israel – otherwise known as gentiles. Here are 3rd Nephi Chapters 29 and 30 from the Book of Mormon:

Book of Mormon, Chapter 29

The coming forth of the Book of Mormon is a sign that the Lord has commenced to gather Israel and fulfill His covenants—Those who reject His latter-day revelations and gifts will be cursed. About A.D. 34-35.

1 And now behold, I say unto you that when the Lord shall see fit, in his wisdom, that these sayings shall come unto the Gentiles according to his word, then ye may know that the covenant which the Father hath made with the children of Israel, concerning their restoration to the lands of their inheritance, is already beginning to be fulfilled.

2 And ye may know that the words of the Lord, which have been spoken by the holy prophets, shall all be fulfilled; and ye need not say that the Lord delays his coming unto the children of Israel.

3 And ye need not imagine in your hearts that the words which have been spoken are vain, for behold, the Lord will remember his covenant which he hath made unto his people of the house of Israel.

4 And when ye shall see these sayings coming forth among you, then ye need not any longer spurn at the doings of the Lord, for the sword of his justice is in his right hand; and behold, at that day, if ye shall spurn at his doings he will cause that it shall soon overtake you.

5 Wo unto him that spurneth at the doings of the Lord; yea, wo unto him that shall deny the Christ and his works!

6 Yea, wo unto him that shall deny the revelations of the Lord, and that shall say the Lord no longer worketh by revelation, or by prophecy, or by gifts, or by tongues, or by healings, or by the power of the Holy Ghost!

7 Yea, and wo unto him that shall say at that day, to get gain, that there can be no miracle wrought by Jesus Christ; for he that doeth this shall become like unto the son of perdition, for whom there was no mercy, according to the word of Christ!

8 Yea, and ye need not any longer hiss, nor spurn, nor make game of the Jews, nor any of the remnant of the house of Israel;

for behold, the Lord remembereth his covenant unto them, and he will do unto them according to that which he hath sworn.

9 Therefore ye need not suppose that ye can turn the right hand of the Lord unto the left, that he may not execute judgment unto the fulfilling of the covenant which he hath made unto the house of Israel.

Book of Mormon, Chapter 30

1 Hearken, O ye Gentiles, and hear the words of Jesus Christ, the Son of the living God, which he hath commanded me that I should speak concerning you, for, behold he commandeth me that I should write, saying:

2 Turn, all ye Gentiles, from your wicked ways; and repent of your evil doings, of your lyings and deceivings, and of your whoredoms, and of your secret abominations, and your idolatries, and of your murders, and your priestcrafts, and your envyings, and your strifes, and from all your wickedness and abominations, and come unto me, and be baptized in my name, that ye may receive a remission of your sins, and be filled with the Holy Ghost, that ye may be numbered with my people who are of the house of Israel.

Now is the time for us to wake up, rise up and start paying attention in this classroom we call Earth. The Lord has called another prophet to usher in the dispensation of the fullness of times in which all things will be revealed to man. The Book of Mormon has been published to the World as another witness that Jesus is the Christ and is proof that our Heavenly Father is preparing to send our Savior back in great glory to rule and reign on the Earth. The ancient Gospel of Jesus Christ has been restored with full Priesthood authority and living prophets to guide us in the church that was named by Jesus himself: The Church of Jesus Christ of Latter-day Saints.

In 1832 the Lord gave the Prophet Joseph Smith a revelation that spells out what must be the future of The Church of Jesus Christ of Latter-day Saints, or Zion as it is referred to in Section 82 of the Doctrine and Covenants:

Section 82

14 For Zion must increase in beauty, and in holiness; her borders must be enlarged; her stakes must be strengthened; yea, verily I say unto you, Zion must arise and put on her beautiful garments.

Since that revelation was published (at a time when the Church was tiny) two years after The Church of Jesus Christ of Latter-day Saints was organized, Zion has indeed strengthened her stakes and put on her beautiful garments. As of December 31, 2021, as reported at the April 2022 General Conference, the Church reported having 3,498 stakes and 31,315 wards and branches (or congregations), with a total membership of 16,805,400. There were 54,539 full-time teaching missionaries and 36,639 Church-Service missionaries.

It is interesting that the Russian writer, Leo Tolstoy, best known as the author of *War and Peace,* showed interest in The Church of Jesus Christ of Latter-day Saints and made a prediction about its future. Count Tolstoy was born in 1828, just two years before The Church of Jesus Christ of Latter-day Saints was organized. When Tolstoy died in 1910, The Church of Jesus Christ of Latter-day Saints had grown to 393,000 members. In 2014, author Susan McCloud, writing for the Deseret News, owned by The Church of Jesus Christ of Latter-day Saints, published her research about Count Tolstoy. Here is part of her article published in the September 21, 2014, Deseret News article "Leo Tolstoy's View of Mormons as Teaching 'The American Religion'" which includes a purported remarkable quote from Tolstoy: ...

> *"What brought Tolstoy to this final statement, if accurate, will, of course, never be known. The absoluteness, the definitive nature of his words, imbues them with a ringing power that sends a thrill through the reader's mind. Given all that Tolstoy was, all that struggled within himself that was unknown to others, his statement on Mormonism [The Church of Jesus Christ of Latter-day Saints] can be considered nothing less than remarkable.*
>
> *According to Yates' account, Tolstoy began by asking [Dr. Andrew D.] White, [President of Cornell University and a former minister to Russia], to tell him of his American religion. White explained that there was no such thing, but Tolstoy persisted, saying, "'I know all of this, but I want to know about the American religion. Catholicism originated in Rome; the Episcopal Church originated in England; the Lutheran Church in Germany, but the Church to which I refer originated in America, and is commonly known as the Mormon Church. What can you tell me of the teachings of the Mormons?'*
>
> *"'Well,' said Dr. White 'I know very little concerning them. They have an unsavory reputation, they practice polygamy, and are very superstitious.'*
>
> *"**Then Count Leo Tolstoy, in his honest and stern, but lovable manner, rebuked the ambassador. 'Dr. White, I am greatly surprised and disappointed that a man of your great learning and position should be so ignorant on this important subject. The Mormon people teach the American religion;***

> *their principles teach the people not only of Heaven and its attendant glories, but how to live so that their social and economic relations with each other are placed on a sound basis. If the people follow the teachings of this Church, nothing can stop their progress — it will be limitless. There have been great movements started in the past but they have died or been modified before they reached maturity. If Mormonism is able to endure, unmodified, until it reaches the third and fourth generation, it is destined to become the greatest power the world has ever known."'*
>
> *Apparently [Dr.] White, after his return home, secured a set of LDS Church works to be placed in the library at Cornell.*
>
> *Notable; extraordinary indeed. We leave these words, as the speaker left them, for your consideration."*

Whether or not the above account was accurately attributed to Tolstoy, so far it has proved to be true. Zion is putting on her beautiful garments, and as the Prophet Joseph Smith reported in 1842 to John Wentworth, Editor of the Chicago Democrat:

> *Our missionaries are going forth to different nations, and in Germany, Palestine, New Holland, Australia, the East Indies, and other places, the Standard of Truth has been erected; no unhallowed hand can stop the work from progressing; persecutions may rage, mobs may combine, armies may assemble, calumny may defame, but the truth of God will go forth boldly, nobly, and independent, till it has penetrated every continent, visited every clime, swept every country, and sounded in every ear; till the purposes of God shall be accomplished, and the Great Jehovah shall say the work is done.*

The Book of Mormon is available to all of our Heavenly Father's children to prove that Jesus is the Christ, the God of the whole Earth, and will soon return in great glory. Zion [The Church of Jesus Christ of Latter-day Saints] will continue to grow in power so that the Gospel can penetrate every continent and nation. All who love the Lord and want to be a part of the great work of preparing for the Savior's return need to read the Book of Mormon as the Prophet Moroni directs – with an honest heart and sincere intent; then ask our Heavenly Father, in the name of Jesus Christ, if it is true. When the Holy Spirit reveals its truth, repentance and baptism must follow along with total commitment to our Lord's cause.

The Book of Mormon is the best kind of proof to convince the honest in heart that God lives, that Jesus is the Christ, and that our Heavenly Father has begun the work of sending His Son back in great glory to rule and reign on the Earth. We can hold the Book of Mormon in our hands. We can learn of an ancient civilization that no one knew existed until the Book of Mormon was published – a civilization that was broken off from Israel in Palestine and transported by ship to the Americas. Along with the physical evidence of the Book of Mormon itself and the witnesses testifying to its truth, we also have the testimony of the Spirit of the Lord. We must all stand before the judgment bar. It is better to be like Paul when he rejected and persecuted the early Christians than to be indifferent and do nothing when the Book of Mormon comes into our hands.

It took me ten years to take seriously the truth of what the Book of Mormon really means to those who are living

in our time: That God lives, that Jesus is the Christ, and that we must build our Lord's Church to receive Him when He returns in great power and glory. It is my hope that the honest in heart - for the honest in heart are those who will be saved at the last day - will not find themselves standing before the bar of the great Jehovah and found by our Savior to be "lukewarm." We must not fail to act when we receive spiritual confirmation that the Book of Mormon is the Word of God. Now is the time to act and follow the Spirit of the Lord with real courage. Our Lord needs us to do our part in preparing the way for His return.

Appendix

Book of Mormon, Ether Chapter 4 -

1 And the Lord commanded the brother of Jared to go down out of the mount from the presence of the Lord, and write the things which he had seen; and they were forbidden to come unto the children of men until after that he should be lifted up upon the cross; and for this cause did king Mosiah keep them, that they should not come unto the world until after Christ should show himself unto his people.

2 And after Christ truly had showed himself unto his people he commanded that they should be made manifest.

3 And now, after that, they have all dwindled in unbelief; and there is none save it be the Lamanites, and they have rejected the gospel of Christ; therefore I am commanded that I should hide them up again in the earth.

4 Behold, I have written upon these plates the very things which the brother of Jared saw; and there never were greater things made manifest than those which were made manifest unto the brother of Jared.

5 Wherefore the Lord hath commanded me to write them; and I have written them. And he commanded me that I should seal them up; and he also hath commanded that I should seal up the interpretation thereof; wherefore I have sealed up the interpreters, according to the commandment of the Lord.

6 For the Lord said unto me: They shall not go forth unto the Gentiles until the day that they shall repent of their iniquity, and become clean before the Lord.

7 And in that day that they shall exercise faith in me, saith the Lord, even as the brother of Jared did, that they may become sanctified in me, then will I manifest unto them the things which the brother of Jared saw, even to the unfolding unto them all my revelations, saith Jesus Christ, the Son of God, the Father of the heavens and of the earth, and all things that in them are.

8 And he that will contend against the word of the Lord, let him be accursed; and he that shall deny these things, let him be accursed; for unto them will I show no greater things, saith Jesus Christ; for I am he who speaketh.

9 And at my command the heavens are opened and are shut; and at my word the earth shall shake; and at my command the inhabitants thereof shall pass away, even so as by fire.

10 And he that believeth not my words believeth not my disciples; and if it so be that I do not speak, judge ye; for ye shall know that it is I that speaketh, at the last day.

11 But he that believeth these things which I have spoken, him will I visit with the manifestations of my Spirit, and he shall know and bear record. For because of my Spirit he shall know that these things are true; for it persuadeth men to do good.

12 And whatsoever thing persuadeth men to do good is of me; for good cometh of none save it be of me. I am the same that leadeth men to all good; he that will not believe my words will not believe me—that I am; and he that will not believe me will not believe the Father who sent me. For behold, I am the Father, I am the light, and the life, and the truth of the world.

13 Come unto me, O ye Gentiles, and I will show unto you the greater things, the knowledge which is hid up because of unbelief.

14 Come unto me, O ye house of Israel, and it shall be made manifest unto you how great things the Father hath laid up for you, from the foundation of the world; and it hath not come unto you, because of unbelief.

15 Behold, when ye shall rend that veil of unbelief which doth cause you to remain in your awful state of wickedness, and hardness of heart, and blindness of mind, then shall the great and marvelous things which have been hid up from the foundation of the world from you—yea, when ye shall call upon the Father in my name, with a broken heart and a contrite spirit, then shall ye know that the Father hath remembered the covenant which he made unto your fathers, O house of Israel.

16 And then shall my revelations which I have caused to be written by my servant John be unfolded in the eyes of all the people. Remember, when ye see these things, ye shall know that the time is at hand that they shall be made manifest in very deed.

17 Therefore, when ye shall receive this record ye may know that the work of the Father has commenced upon all the face of the land.

18 Therefore, repent all ye ends of the earth, and come unto me, and believe in my gospel, and be baptized in my name; for he that believeth and is baptized shall be saved; but he that believeth not shall be damned; and signs shall follow them that believe in my name.

19 And blessed is he that is found faithful unto my name at the last day, for he shall be lifted up to dwell in the kingdom prepared for him from the foundation of the world. And behold it is I that hath spoken it. Amen

NOTE 2 FROM CHAPTER ONE .... pg 18

Moroni 10:

1 Now I, Moroni, write somewhat as seemeth me good; and I write unto my brethren, the Lamanites; and I would that they should know that more than four hundred and twenty years have passed away since the sign was given of the coming of Christ. 2 And I seal up these records, after I have spoken a few words by way of exhortation unto you.

3 Behold, I would exhort you that when ye shall read these things, if it be wisdom in God that ye should read them, that ye would remember how merciful the Lord hath been unto the children of men, from the creation of Adam even down until the time that ye shall receive these things, and ponder it in your hearts. 4 And when ye shall receive these things, I would exhort you that ye would ask God, the Eternal Father, in the name of Christ, if these things are not true; and if ye shall ask with a sincere heart, with real intent, having faith in Christ, he will manifest the truth of it unto you, by the power of the Holy Ghost. 5 And by the power of the Holy Ghost ye may know the truth of all things.

6 And whatsoever thing is good is just and true; wherefore, nothing that is good denieth the Christ, but acknowledgeth that he is. 7 And ye may know that he is, by the power of the Holy Ghost; wherefore I would exhort you that ye deny not the power of God; for he worketh by power, according to the faith of the children of men, the same today and tomorrow, and forever.

8 And again, I exhort you, my brethren, that ye deny not the gifts of God, for they are many; and they come from the same God. And there are different ways that these gifts are administered; but it is the same God who worketh all in all; and they are given by the manifestations of the Spirit of God unto men, to profit them. 9 For behold, to one is given by the Spirit of God, that he may teach the word of wisdom;

10 And to another, that he may teach the word of knowledge by the same Spirit;

11 And to another, exceedingly great faith; and to another, the gifts of healing by the same Spirit;

12 And again, to another, that he may work mighty miracles;

13 And again, to another, that he may prophesy concerning all things;

14 And again, to another, the beholding of angels and ministering spirits;

15 And again, to another, all kinds of tongues;

16 And again, to another, the interpretation of languages and of divers kinds of tongues.

17 And all these gifts come by the Spirit of Christ; and they come unto every man severally, according as he will. 18 And I would exhort you, my beloved brethren, that ye remember that every good gift cometh of Christ. 19 And I would exhort you, my beloved brethren, that ye remember that he is the same yesterday, today, and forever, and that all these gifts of which I have spoken, which are spiritual, never will be done away, even as long as the world shall stand, only according to the unbelief of the children of men.

20 Wherefore, there must be faith; and if there must be faith there must also be hope; and if there must be hope there must also be charity. 21 And except ye have charity ye can in nowise be saved in the kingdom of God; neither can ye be saved in the kingdom of God if ye have not faith; neither can ye if ye have no hope. 22 And if ye have no hope ye must needs be in despair; and despair cometh because of iniquity.

23 And Christ truly said unto our fathers: If ye have faith ye can do all things which are expedient unto me.

24 And now I speak unto all the ends of the earth—that if the day cometh that the power and gifts of God shall be done away among you, it shall be because of unbelief. 25 And wo be unto the children of men if this be the case; for there shall be none that doeth good among you, no not one. For if there be one among you that doeth good, he shall work by the power and gifts of God. 26 And wo unto them who shall do these things away and die, for they die in their sins, and they cannot be saved in the kingdom of God; and I speak it according to the words of Christ; and I lie not.

27 And I exhort you to remember these things; for the time speedily cometh that ye shall know that I lie not, for ye shall see me at the bar of God; and the Lord God will say unto you: Did I not declare my words unto you, which were written by this man, like as one crying from the dead, yea, even as one speaking out of the dust?

28 I declare these things unto the fulfilling of the prophecies. And behold, they shall proceed forth out of the mouth of the everlasting God; and his word shall hiss forth from generation to generation.

29 And God shall show unto you, that that which I have written is true.

30 And again I would exhort you that ye would come unto Christ, and lay hold upon every good gift, and touch not the evil gift, nor the unclean thing. 31 And awake, and arise from the dust, O Jerusalem; yea, and put on thy beautiful garments, O daughter of Zion; and strengthen thy stakes and enlarge thy borders forever, that thou mayest no more be confounded, that the covenants of the Eternal Father which he hath made unto thee, O house of Israel, may be fulfilled.

32 Yea, come unto Christ, and be perfected in him, and deny yourselves of all ungodliness; and if ye shall deny yourselves of all ungodliness, and love God with all your might, mind and strength, then is his grace sufficient for you, that by his grace ye may be perfect in Christ; and if by the grace of God ye are perfect in Christ, ye can in nowise deny the power of God.

33 And again, if ye by the grace of God are perfect in Christ, and deny not his power, then are ye sanctified in Christ by the grace of God, through the shedding of the blood of Christ, which is in the covenant of the Father unto the remission of your sins, that ye become holy, without spot.

34 And now I bid unto all, farewell. I soon go to rest in the paradise of God, until my spirit and body shall again reunite, and I am brought forth triumphant through the air, to meet you before the pleasing bar of the great Jehovah, the Eternal Judge of both quick and dead. Amen

NOTE 3 FROM CHAPTER TWO .... pg 27

Pearl of Great Price, Joseph Smith - History:

Oliver Cowdery describes these events thus: "These were days never to be forgotten—to sit under the sound of a voice dictated by the inspiration of heaven, awakened the utmost gratitude of this bosom! Day after day I continued, uninterrupted, to write from his mouth, as he translated with the Urim and Thummim, or, as the Nephites would have said, 'Interpreters,' the history or record called 'The Book of Mormon.' "To notice, in even few words, the interesting account given by Mormon and his faithful son, Moroni, of a people once beloved and favored of heaven, would supersede my present design; I shall therefore defer this to a future period, and, as I said in the introduction, pass more directly to some few incidents immediately connected with the rise of this Church, which may be entertaining to some thousands who have stepped forward, amid the frowns of bigots and the calumny of hypocrites, and embraced the Gospel of Christ.

"No men, in their sober senses, could translate and write the directions given to the Nephites from the mouth of the Savior, of the precise manner in which men should build up His Church, and especially when corruption had spread an uncertainty over all forms and systems practiced among men, without desiring a privilege of showing the willingness of the heart by being buried in the liquid

grave, to answer a 'good conscience by the resurrection of Jesus Christ.'

"After writing the account given of the Savior's ministry to the remnant of the seed of Jacob, upon this continent, it was easy to be seen, as the prophet said it would be, that darkness covered the earth and gross darkness the minds of the people. On reflecting further it was as easy to be seen that amid the great strife and noise concerning religion, none had authority from God to administer the ordinances of the Gospel.

For the question might be asked, have men authority to administer in the name of Christ, who deny revelations, when His testimony is no less than the spirit of prophecy, and His religion based, built, and sustained by immediate revelations, in all ages of the world when He has had a people on earth?

If these facts were buried, and carefully concealed by men whose craft would have been in danger if once permitted to shine in the faces of men, they were no longer to us; and we only waited for the commandment to be given 'Arise and be baptized.'

"This was not long desired before it was realized. The Lord, who is rich in mercy, and ever willing to answer the consistent prayer of the humble, after we had called upon Him in a fervent manner, aside from the abodes of men, condescended to manifest to us His will.

On a sudden, as from the midst of eternity, the voice of the Redeemer spake peace to us, while the veil was parted and the angel of God came down clothed with glory, and delivered the anxiously looked for message, and the keys of the Gospel of repentance.

What joy! what wonder! what amazement! While the world was racked and distracted —while millions were groping as the blind for the wall, and while all men were resting upon uncertainty, as a general mass, our eyes beheld, our ears heard, as in the 'blaze of day'; yes, more—above the glitter of the May sunbeam, which then shed its brilliancy over the face of nature!

Then his voice, though mild, pierced to the center, and his words, 'I am thy fellow-servant,' dispelled every fear. We listened, we gazed, we admired! 'Twas the voice of an angel from glory, 'twas a message from the Most High! And as we heard we rejoiced, while His love enkindled upon our souls, and we were wrapped in the vision of the Almighty!

Where was room for doubt? Nowhere; uncertainty had fled, doubt had sunk no more to rise, while fiction and deception had fled forever! "But, dear brother, think, further think for a moment, what joy filled our hearts, and with what surprise we must have bowed, (for who would not have bowed the knee for such a blessing?) when we received under his hand the Holy Priesthood as he said, 'Upon you my fellow-servants, in the name of Messiah, I confer this Priesthood and this authority, which shall remain upon earth, that the Sons of Levi may yet offer an offering unto the Lord in righteousness!'

"I shall not attempt to paint to you the feelings of this heart, nor the majestic beauty and glory which surrounded us on this occasion; but you will believe me when I say, that earth, nor men, with the eloquence of time, cannot begin to clothe language in as interesting and sublime a manner as this holy personage.

No; nor has this earth power to give the joy, to bestow the peace, or comprehend the wisdom which was contained in each sentence as they were delivered by the power of the Holy Spirit!

Man may deceive his fellow-men, deception may follow deception, and the children of the wicked one may have power to seduce the foolish and untaught, till naught but fiction feeds the many, and the fruit of falsehood carries in its current the giddy to the grave; but one touch with the finger of his love, yes, one ray of glory from the upper world, or one word from the mouth of the Savior, from the bosom of eternity, strikes it all into insignificance, and blots it forever from the mind.

The assurance that we were in the presence of an angel, the certainty that we heard the voice of Jesus, and the truth unsullied as it flowed from a pure personage, dictated by the will of God, is to me past description, and I shall ever look upon this expression of the Savior's goodness with wonder and thanksgiving while I am permitted to tarry; and in those mansions where perfection dwells and sin never comes, I hope to adore in that day which shall never cease."—Messenger and Advocate, vol. 1 (October 1834), pp. 14–16.

NOTE 4 FROM CHAPTER THREE .... pg 34

3 Nephi 15

10. Behold, I have given unto you the commandments; therefore keep my commandments. And this is the law and the prophets, for they truly testified of me. 11 And now it came to pass that when Jesus had spoken these words, he said unto those twelve whom he had chosen: 12 Ye are my disciples; and ye are a light unto this people, who are a remnant of the house of Joseph. 13 And behold, this is the land of your inheritance; and the Father hath given it unto you. 14 And not at any time hath the Father given me commandment that I should tell it unto your brethren at Jerusalem. 15 Neither at any time hath the Father given me commandment that I should tell unto them concerning the other tribes of the house of Israel, whom the Father hath led away out of the land. 16 This much did the Father command me, that I should tell unto them: 17 That other sheep I have which are not of this fold; them also I must bring, and they shall hear my voice; and there shall be one fold, and one shepherd. 18 And now, because of stiffneckedness and unbelief they understood not my word; therefore I was commanded to say no more of the Father concerning this thing unto them. 19 But, verily, I say unto you that the Father hath commanded me, and I tell it unto you, that ye were separated from among them because of their iniquity; therefore it is because of their iniquity that they know not of you. 20 And verily, I say unto you again that the other tribes

hath the Father separated from them; and it is because of their iniquity that they know not of them. 21 **And verily I say unto you, that ye are they of whom I said: Other sheep I have which are not of this fold; them also I must bring, and they shall hear my voice; and there shall be one fold, and one shepherd.** 22 And they understood me not, for they supposed it had been the Gentiles; for they understood not that the Gentiles should be converted through their preaching. 23 And they understood me not that I said they shall hear my voice; and they understood me not that the Gentiles should not at any time hear my voice—that I should not manifest myself unto them save it were by the Holy Ghost. 24 But behold, ye have both heard my voice, and seen me; and ye are my sheep, and ye are numbered among those whom the Father hath given me.

NOTE 5 FROM CHAPTER THREE .... pg 36

3 Nephi 21

CHAPTER 21 Israel will be gathered when the Book of Mormon comes forth—The Gentiles will be established as a free people in America—They will be saved if they believe and obey; otherwise, they will be cut off and destroyed—Israel will build the New Jerusalem, and the lost tribes will return. About A.D. 34.

1 And verily I say unto you, I give unto you a sign, that ye may know the time when these things shall be about to take place—that I shall gather in, from their long dispersion, my people, O house of Israel, and shall establish again among them my Zion;

2 And behold, this is the thing which I will give unto you for a sign—for verily I say unto you that when these things which I declare unto you, and which I shall declare unto you hereafter of myself, and by the power of the Holy Ghost which shall be given unto you of the Father, shall be made known unto the Gentiles that they may know concerning this people who are a remnant of the house of Jacob, and concerning this my people who shall be scattered by them;

3 Verily, verily, I say unto you, when these things shall be made known unto them of the Father, and shall come forth of the Father, from them unto you;

4 For it is wisdom in the Father that they should be established in this land, and be set up as a free people by the power of the Father, that these things might come forth from them unto a remnant of your seed, that the covenant of the Father may be fulfilled which he hath covenanted with his people, O house of Israel;

5 Therefore, when these works and the works which shall be wrought among you hereafter shall come forth from the Gentiles, unto your seed which shall dwindle in unbelief because of iniquity;

6 For thus it behooveth the Father that it should come forth from the Gentiles, that he may show forth his power unto the Gentiles, for this cause that the Gentiles, if they will not harden their hearts, that they may repent and come unto me and be baptized in my name and know of the true points of my doctrine, that they may be numbered among my people, O house of Israel;

7 And when these things come to pass that thy seed shall begin to know these things—it shall be a sign unto them, that they may know that the work of the Father hath already commenced unto the fulfilling of the covenant which he hath made unto the people who are of the house of Israel.

8 And when that day shall come, it shall come to pass that kings shall shut their mouths; for that which had not been told them shall they see; and that which they had not heard shall they consider.

9 For in that day, for my sake shall the Father work a work, which shall be a great and a marvelous work among them; and there shall be among them those who will not believe it, although a man shall declare it unto them.

10 But behold, the life of my servant shall be in my hand; therefore they shall not hurt him, although he shall be marred because of them. Yet I will heal him, for I will show unto them that my wisdom is greater than the cunning of the devil.

11 Therefore it shall come to pass that whosoever will not believe in my words, who am Jesus Christ, which the Father shall cause him to bring forth unto the Gentiles, and shall give unto him power that he shall bring them forth unto the Gentiles, (it shall be done even as Moses said) they shall be cut off from among my people who are of the covenant.

12 And my people who are a remnant of Jacob shall be among the Gentiles, yea, in the midst of them as a lion among the beasts of the forest, as a young lion among the flocks of sheep, who, if he go through both treadeth down and teareth in pieces, and none can deliver.

13 Their hand shall be lifted up upon their adversaries, and all their enemies shall be cut off. 14 Yea, wo be unto the Gentiles except they repent; for it shall come to pass in that day, saith the Father, that I will cut off thy horses out of the midst of thee, and I will destroy thy chariots;

15 And I will cut off the cities of thy land, and throw down all thy strongholds; 16 And I will cut off witchcrafts out of thy land, and thou shalt have no more soothsayers; 17 Thy graven images I will also cut off, and thy standing images out of the midst of thee, and thou shalt no more worship the works of thy hands;

18 And I will pluck up thy groves out of the midst of thee; so will I destroy thy cities.

19 And it shall come to pass that all lyings, and deceivings, and envyings, and strifes, and priestcrafts, and whoredoms, shall be done away.

20 For it shall come to pass, saith the Father, that at that day whosoever will not repent and come unto my Beloved Son, them will I cut off from among my people, O house of Israel;

21 And I will execute vengeance and fury upon them, even as upon the heathen, such as they have not heard.

22 But if they will repent and hearken unto my words, and harden not their hearts, I will establish my church among them, and they shall come in unto the covenant and be numbered among this the remnant of Jacob, unto whom I have given this land for their inheritance;

23 And they shall assist my people, the remnant of Jacob, and also as many of the house of Israel as shall come, that they may build a city, which shall be called the New Jerusalem.

24 And then shall they assist my people that they may be gathered in, who are scattered upon all the face of the land, in unto the New Jerusalem.

25 And then shall the power of heaven come down among them; and I also will be in the midst.

26 And then shall the work of the Father commence at that day, even when this gospel shall be preached among the remnant of this people. Verily I say unto you, at that day shall the work of the Father commence among all the dispersed of my people, yea, even the tribes which have been lost, which the Father hath led away out of Jerusalem.

27 Yea, the work shall commence among all the dispersed of my people, with the Father to prepare the way whereby they may come unto me, that they may call on the Father in my name.

28 Yea, and then shall the work commence, with the Father among all nations in preparing the way whereby his people may be gathered home to the land of their inheritance.

29 And they shall go out from all nations; and they shall not go out in haste, nor go by flight, for I will go before them, saith the Father, and I will be their rearward.

NOTE 6 FROM CHAPTER THREE .... pg 37

3 Nephi 8:

3 And the people began to look with great earnestness for the sign which had been given by the prophet Samuel, the Lamanite, yea, for the time that there should be darkness for the space of three days over the face of the land.

4 And there began to be great doubtings and disputations among the people, notwithstanding so many signs had been given.

5 And it came to pass in the thirty and fourth year, in the first month, on the fourth day of the month, there arose a great storm, such an one as never had been known in all the land.

6 And there was also a great and terrible tempest; and there was terrible thunder, insomuch that it did shake the whole earth as if it was about to divide asunder.

7 And there were exceedingly sharp lightnings, such as never had been known in all the land. 8 And the city of Zarahemla did take fire. 9 And the city of Moroni did sink into the depths of the sea, and the inhabitants thereof were drowned.

10 And the earth was carried up upon the city of Moronihah, that in the place of the city there became a great mountain. 11 And there was a great and terrible destruction in the land southward.

12 But behold, there was a more great and terrible destruction in the land northward; for behold, the whole face of the land was changed, because of the tempest and the whirlwinds, and the thunderings and the lightnings, and the exceedingly great quaking of the whole earth;

13 And the highways were broken up, and the level roads were spoiled, and many smooth places became rough.

14 And many great and notable cities were sunk, and many were burned, and many were shaken till the buildings thereof had fallen to the earth, and the inhabitants thereof were slain, and the places were left desolate.

15 And there were some cities which remained; but the damage thereof was exceedingly great, and there were many in them who were slain.

16 And there were some who were carried away in the whirlwind; and whither they went no man knoweth, save they know that they were carried away.

17 And thus the face of the whole earth became deformed, because of the tempests, and the thunderings, and the lightnings, and the quaking of the earth.

18 And behold, the rocks were rent in twain; they were broken up upon the face of the whole earth, insomuch that they were found in broken fragments, and in seams and in cracks, upon all the face of the land.

19 And it came to pass that when the thunderings, and the lightnings, and the storm, and the tempest, and the quakings of the earth did cease—for behold, they did last for about the space of three hours; and it was said by some that the time was greater; nevertheless, all these great and terrible things were done in about the space of three hours—and then behold, there was darkness upon the face of the land.

20 And it came to pass that there was thick darkness upon all the face of the land, insomuch that the inhabitants thereof who had not fallen could feel the vapor of darkness;

21 And there could be no light, because of the darkness, neither candles, neither torches; neither could there be fire kindled with their fine and exceedingly dry wood, so that there could not be any light at all;

22 And there was not any light seen, neither fire, nor glimmer, neither the sun, nor the moon, nor the stars, for so great were the mists of darkness which were upon the face of the land.

23 And it came to pass that it did last for the space of three days that there was no light seen; and there was great mourning and howling and weeping among all the people continually; yea, great were the groanings of the people, because of the darkness and the great destruction which had come upon them.

24 And in one place they were heard to cry, saying: O that we had repented before this great and terrible day, and then would our brethren have been spared, and they would not have been burned in that great city Zarahemla.

25 And in another place they were heard to cry and mourn, saying: O that we had repented before this great and terrible day, and had not killed and stoned the prophets, and cast them out; then would our mothers and our fair daughters, and our children have been spared, and not have been buried up in that great city Moronihah. And thus were the howlings of the people great and terrible.

NOTE 7 CHAPTER THREE .... pg 37

Prayer of Orson Hyde on the Mount of Olives – October 24, 1841

"O Thou! who art from everlasting to everlasting, eternally and unchangeably the same, even the God who rules in the heavens above, and controls the destinies of men on the earth, wilt Thou not condescend, through thine infinite goodness and royal favor, to listen to the prayer of Thy servant which he this day offers up unto Thee in the name of Thy holy child Jesus, upon this land, where the Son of Righteousness set in blood, and thine Anointed One expired.

"Be pleased, O Lord, to forgive all the follies, weaknesses, vanities, and sins of Thy servant, and strengthen him to resist all future temptations. Give him prudence and discernment that he may avoid the evil, and a heart to choose the good; give him fortitude to bear up under trying and adverse circumstances, and grace to endure all things for Thy name's sake, until the end shall come, when all the Saints shall rest in peace.

"Now, O Lord! Thy servant has been obedient to the heavenly vision which Thou gavest him in his native land; and under the shadow of Thine outstretched arm, he has safely arrived in this place to dedicate and consecrate this land unto Thee, for the gathering together of Judah's scattered remnants, according to the predictions of the holy Prophets — for the building up of Jerusalem again after it has been trodden down by the Gentiles so long, and for rearing a Temple in honor of Thy name. Everlasting thanks be ascribed unto Thee, O Father, Lord of heaven and earth, that Thou hast preserved Thy servant from the dangers of the seas, and from the plague and pestilence which have caused the land to mourn. The violence of man has also been restrained, and Thy providential care by night and by day has been exercised over Thine unworthy servant. Accept, therefore, O Lord, the tribute of a grateful heart for all past favors, and be pleased to continue Thy kindness and mercy towards a needy worm of the dust.

"O Thou, Who didst covenant with Abraham, Thy friend, and who didst renew that covenant with Isaac, and confirm the same with Jacob with an oath, that Thou wouldst not only give them this land for an everlasting inheritance, but that Thou wouldst also remember their seed forever. Abraham, Isaac, and Jacob have long since closed their eyes in death, and made the grave their mansion. Their children are scattered and dispersed abroad among the nations of the Gentiles like sheep that have no shepherd, and are still looking forward for the fulfillment of those promises which Thou didst make concerning them; and even this land, which once poured forth nature's richest bounty, and flowed, as it were, with milk and *honey, has, to a certain extent, been smitten with barrenness and sterility since it drank from murderous hands the blood of Him who never sinned.*

"Grant, therefore, O Lord, in the name of Thy well-beloved Son, Jesus Christ, to remove the barrenness and sterility of this land, and let springs of living water break forth to water its thirsty soil. Let the vine and olive produce in their strength, and the fig-tree bloom and flourish. Let the land become abundantly fruitful when possessed by its rightful heirs; let it again flow with plenty to feed the returning prodigals who come home with a spirit of grace and supplication; upon it let the clouds distil virtue and richness, and let the fields smile with plenty. Let the flocks and the herds greatly increase and multiply upon the mountains and the hills; and let Thy great kindness conquer and subdue the unbelief of Thy people. Do Thou take from them their stony heart, and give them a heart of flesh; and may the Sun of Thy favor dispel the cold mists of darkness which have beclouded their atmosphere. Incline them to gather in upon this land according to Thy word. Let them come like clouds and like doves to their windows. Let the large ships of the nations bring them from the distant isles; and let kings become their nursing fathers, and queens with motherly fondness wipe the tear of sorrow from their eye.

"Thou, O Lord, did once move upon the heart of Cyrus to show favor unto Jerusalem and her children. Do Thou now also be pleased to inspire the hearts of kings and the powers of the earth to look with a friendly eye towards this place, and with a desire to see Thy righteous purposes executed in relation thereto. Let them know that it is Thy good pleasure to restore the kingdom unto Israel — raise up Jerusalem as its capital, and constitute her people a distinct nation and government, with David Thy servant, even a descendant from the loins of ancient David to be their king.

"Let that nation or that people who shall take an active part in behalf of Abraham's children, and in the raising up of Jerusalem, find favor in Thy sight. Let not their enemies prevail against them,

neither let pestilence or famine overcome them, but let the glory of Israel overshadow them, and the power of the Highest protect them; while that nation or kingdom that will not serve Thee in this glorious work must perish, according to Thy word — Yea, those nations shall be utterly wasted.

"Though Thy servant is now far from his home, and from the land bedewed with his earliest tear, yet he remembers, O Lord, his friend: who are there, and family, whom for Thy sake he has left. Though poverty and privation be our earthly lot, yet ah! do Thou richly endow us with an inheritance where moth and rust do not corrupt, and where thieves do not break through and steal.

"The hands that have fed, clothed, or shown favor unto the family of Thy servant in his absence, or that shall hereafter do so, let them not lose their reward, but let a special blessing rest upon them, and in Thy kingdom let them have an inheritance when Thou shalt come to be glorified in this society.

"Do Thou also look with favor upon all those through whose liberality I have been enabled to come to this land; and in the day when Thou shalt reward all people according to their works, let these also not be passed by or forgotten, but in time let them be in readiness to enjoy the glory of those mansions which Jesus has gone to prepare. Particularly do Thou bless the stranger in Philadelphia, whom I never saw, but who sent me gold, with a request that I should pray for him in Jerusalem. Now, O Lord, let blessings come upon him from an unexpected quarter, and let his basket be filled, and his storehouse abound with plenty, and let not the good things of the earth be his only portion, but let him be found among those to whom it shall be said, `Thou hast been faithful over a few things, and I will make thee ruler over many.'

"O my Father in heaven! I now ask Thee in the name of Jesus to remember Zion, with all her Stakes, and with all her assemblies. She has been grievously afflicted and smitten; she has mourned; she has wept; her enemies have triumphed, and have said, `Ah, where

is thy God?' Her Priests and Prophets have groaned in chains and fetters within the gloomy walls of prisons, while many were slain, and now sleep in the arms of death. How long, O Lord, shall iniquity triumph, and sin go unpunished?

"Do Thou arise in the majesty of Thy strength, and make bare Thine arm in behalf of Thy people. Redress their wrongs, and turn their sorrow into joy. Pour the spirit of light and knowledge, grace and wisdom, into the hearts of her Prophets, and clothe her Priests with salvation. Let light and knowledge march forth through the empire of darkness, and may the honest in heart flow to their standard, and join in the march to go forth to meet the Bridegroom.

"Let a peculiar blessing rest upon the Presidency of Thy Church, for at them are the arrows of the enemy directed. Be Thou to them a sun and a shield, their strong tower and hiding place; and in the time of distress or danger be Thou near to deliver. Also the quorum of the Twelve, do Thou be pleased to stand by them for Thou knowest the obstacles which they have to encounter, the temptations to which they are exposed, and the privations which they must suffer. Give us, [the Twelve] therefore, strength according to our day, and help us to bear a faithful testimony of Jesus and His Gospel, to finish with fidelity and honor the work which Thou hast given us to do, and then give us a place in Thy glorious kingdom. And let this blessing rest upon every faithful officer and member in Thy Church. And all the glory and honor will we ascribe unto God and the Lamb forever and ever. Amen."

NOTE 8 CHAPTER 4 .... pg 46

The prophecy of Samuel, the Lamanite, to the Nephites. Comprising chapters 13 through 15:

The Book of Mormon, Helaman Chapter 13

Samuel the Lamanite prophesies the destruction of the Nephites unless they repent—They and their riches are cursed—They reject *and stone the prophets, are encircled about by demons, and seek for happiness in doing iniquity. About 6 B.C.*

1 And now it came to pass in the eighty and sixth year, the Nephites did still remain in wickedness, yea, in great wickedness, while the Lamanites did observe strictly to keep the commandments of God, according to the law of Moses.

2 And it came to pass that in this year there was one Samuel, a Lamanite, came into the land of Zarahemla, and began to preach unto the people. And it came to pass that he did preach, many days, repentance unto the people, and they did cast him out, and he was about to return to his own land.

3 But behold, the voice of the Lord came unto him, that he should return again, and prophesy unto the people whatsoever things should come into his heart.

4 And it came to pass that they would not suffer that he should enter into the city; therefore he went and got upon the wall thereof, and stretched forth his hand and cried with a loud voice, and prophesied unto the people whatsoever things the Lord put into his heart.

5 And he said unto them: Behold, I, Samuel, a Lamanite, do speak the words of the Lord which he doth put into my heart; and behold he hath put it into my heart to say unto this people that the sword of justice hangeth over this people; and four hundred years pass not away save the sword of justice falleth upon this people.

6 Yea, heavy destruction awaiteth this people, and it surely cometh unto this people, and nothing can save this people save it be repentance and faith on the Lord Jesus Christ, who surely shall come into the world, and shall suffer many things and shall be slain for his people.

7 And behold, an angel of the Lord hath declared it unto me, and he did bring glad tidings to my soul. And behold, I was sent unto

you to declare it unto you also, that ye might have glad tidings; but behold ye would not receive me.

8 *Therefore, thus saith the Lord: Because of the hardness of the hearts of the people of the Nephites, except they repent I will take away my word from them, and I will withdraw my Spirit from them, and I will suffer them no longer, and I will turn the hearts of their brethren against them.*

9 *And four hundred years shall not pass away before I will cause that they shall be smitten; yea, I will visit them with the sword and with famine and with pestilence.*

10 *Yea, I will visit them in my fierce anger, and there shall be those of the fourth generation who shall live, of your enemies, to behold your utter destruction; and this shall surely come except ye repent, saith the Lord; and those of the fourth generation shall visit your destruction.*

11 *But if ye will repent and return unto the Lord your God I will turn away mine anger, saith the Lord; yea, thus saith the Lord, blessed are they who will repent and turn unto me, but wo unto him that repenteth not.*

12 *Yea, wo unto this great city of Zarahemla; for behold, it is because of those who are righteous that it is saved; yea, wo unto this great city, for I perceive, saith the Lord, that there are many, yea, even the more part of this great city, that will harden their hearts against me, saith the Lord.*

13 *But blessed are they who will repent, for them will I spare. But behold, if it were not for the righteous who are in this great city, behold, I would cause that fire should come down out of heaven and destroy it.*

14 *But behold, it is for the righteous' sake that it is spared. But behold, the time cometh, saith the Lord, that when ye shall cast out the righteous from among you, then shall ye be ripe for destruction;*

yea, wo be unto this great city, because of the wickedness and abominations which are in her.

15 Yea, and wo be unto the city of Gideon, for the wickedness and abominations which are in her.

16 Yea, and wo be unto all the cities which are in the land round about, which are possessed by the Nephites, because of the wickedness and abominations which are in them.

17 And behold, a curse shall come upon the land, saith the Lord of Hosts, because of the people's sake who are upon the land, yea, because of their wickedness and their abominations.

The Book of Mormon, Helaman Chapter 14

Samuel predicts light during the night and a new star at Christ's birth—Christ redeems men from temporal and spiritual death—The signs of His death include three days of darkness, the rending of the rocks, and great upheavals of nature. About 6 B.C.

1 And now it came to pass that Samuel, the Lamanite, did prophesy a great many more things which cannot be written.

2 And behold, he said unto them: Behold, I give unto you a sign; for five years more cometh, and behold, then cometh the Son of God to redeem all those who shall believe on his name.

3 And behold, this will I give unto you for a sign at the time of his coming; for behold, there shall be great lights in heaven, insomuch that in the night before he cometh there shall be no darkness, insomuch that it shall appear unto man as if it was day.

4 Therefore, there shall be one day and a night and a day, as if it were one day and there were no night; and this shall be unto you for a sign; for ye shall know of the rising of the sun and also of its setting; therefore they shall know of a surety that there shall be two days and a night; nevertheless the night shall not be darkened; and it shall be the night before he is born.

5 And behold, there shall a new star arise, such an one as ye never have beheld; and this also shall be a sign unto you.

6 And behold this is not all, there shall be many signs and wonders in heaven.

7 And it shall come to pass that ye shall all be amazed, and wonder, insomuch that ye shall fall to the earth.

8 And it shall come to pass that whosoever shall believe on the Son of God, the same shall have everlasting life.

9 And behold, thus hath the Lord commanded me, by his angel, that I should come and tell this thing unto you; yea, he hath commanded that I should prophesy these things unto you; yea, he hath said unto me: Cry unto this people, repent and prepare the way of the Lord.

10 And now, because I am a Lamanite, and have spoken unto you the words which the Lord hath commanded me, and because it was hard against you, ye are angry with me and do seek to destroy me, and have cast me out from among you.

11 And ye shall hear my words, for, for this intent have I come up upon the walls of this city, that ye might hear and know of the judgments of God which do await you because of your iniquities, and also that ye might know the conditions of repentance;

12 And also that ye might know of the coming of Jesus Christ, the Son of God, the Father of heaven and of earth, the Creator of all things from the beginning; and that ye might know of the signs of his coming, to the intent that ye might believe on his name.

13 And if ye believe on his name ye will repent of all your sins, that thereby ye may have a remission of them through his merits.

14 And behold, again, another sign I give unto you, yea, a sign of his death.

15 For behold, he surely must die that salvation may come; yea, it behooveth him and becometh expedient that he dieth, to bring to pass the resurrection of the dead, that thereby men may be brought into the presence of the Lord.

16 Yea, behold, this death bringeth to pass the resurrection, and redeemeth all mankind from the first death—that spiritual death; for all mankind, by the fall of Adam being cut off from the presence of the Lord, are considered as dead, both as to things temporal and to things spiritual.

17 But behold, the resurrection of Christ redeemeth mankind, yea, even all mankind, and bringeth them back into the presence of the Lord.

18 Yea, and it bringeth to pass the condition of repentance, that whosoever repenteth the same is not hewn down and cast into the fire; but whosoever repenteth not is hewn down and cast into the fire; and there cometh upon them again a spiritual death, yea, a second death, for they are cut off again as to things pertaining to righteousness.

19 Therefore repent ye, repent ye, lest by knowing these things and not doing them ye shall suffer yourselves to come under condemnation, and ye are brought down unto this second death.

20 But behold, as I said unto you concerning another sign, a sign of his death, behold, in that day that he shall suffer death the sun shall be darkened and refuse to give his light unto you; and also the moon and the stars; and there shall be no light upon the face of this land, even from the time that he shall suffer death, for the space of three days, to the time that he shall rise again from the dead.

21 Yea, at the time that he shall yield up the ghost there shall be thunderings and lightnings for the space of many hours, and the earth shall shake and tremble; and the rocks which are upon the face of this earth, which are both above the earth and beneath, which ye know at this time are solid, or the more part of it is one solid mass, shall be broken up;

22 Yea, they shall be rent in twain, and shall ever after be found in seams and in cracks, and in broken fragments upon the face of the whole earth, yea, both above the earth and beneath.

23 And behold, there shall be great tempests, and there shall be many mountains laid low, like unto a valley, and there shall be many places which are now called valleys which shall become mountains, whose height is great.

24 And many highways shall be broken up, and many cities shall become desolate. 25 And many graves shall be opened, and shall yield up many of their dead; and many saints shall appear unto many.

26 And behold, thus hath the angel spoken unto me; for he said unto me that there should be thunderings and lightnings for the space of many hours.

27 And he said unto me that while the thunder and the lightning lasted, and the tempest, that these things should be, and that darkness should cover the face of the whole earth for the space of three days.

28 And the angel said unto me that many shall see greater things than these, to the intent that they might believe that these signs and these wonders should come to pass upon all the face of this land, to the intent that there should be no cause for unbelief among the children of men—

29 And this to the intent that whosoever will believe might be saved, and that whosoever will not believe, a righteous judgment might come upon them; and also if they are condemned they bring upon themselves their own condemnation.

30 And now remember, remember, my brethren, that whosoever perisheth, perisheth unto himself; and whosoever doeth iniquity, doeth it unto himself; for behold, ye are free; ye are permitted to act for yourselves; for behold, God hath given unto you a knowledge and he hath made you free.

31 He hath given unto you that ye might know good from evil, and he hath given unto you that ye might choose life or death; and ye can do good and be restored unto that which is good, or have that which is good restored unto you; or ye can do evil, and have that which is evil restored unto you.

The Book of Mormon, Helaman Chapter 15

The Lord chastened the Nephites because He loved them—Converted Lamanites are firm and steadfast in the faith—The Lord will be merciful unto the Lamanites in the latter days. About 6 B.C.

4 But behold my brethren, the Lamanites hath he hated because their deeds have been evil continually, and this because of the iniquity of the tradition of their fathers. But behold, salvation hath come unto them through the preaching of the Nephites; and for this intent hath the Lord prolonged their days.

12 Yea, I say unto you, that in the latter times the promises of the Lord have been extended to our brethren, the Lamanites; and notwithstanding the many afflictions which they shall have, and notwithstanding they shall be driven to and fro upon the face of the earth, and be hunted, and shall be smitten and scattered abroad, having no place for refuge, the Lord shall be merciful unto them.

13 And this is according to the prophecy, that they shall again be brought to the true knowledge, which is the knowledge of their Redeemer, and their great and true shepherd, and be numbered among his sheep.

14 Therefore I say unto you, it shall be better for them than for you except ye repent.

15 For behold, had the mighty works been shown unto them which have been shown unto you, yea, unto them who have dwindled in unbelief because of the traditions of their fathers, ye can see of yourselves that they never would again have dwindled in unbelief.

16 Therefore, saith the Lord: I will not utterly destroy them, but I will cause that in the day of my wisdom they shall return again unto me, saith the Lord.

17 And now behold, saith the Lord, concerning the people of the Nephites: If they will not repent, and observe to do my will, I will utterly destroy them, saith the Lord, because of their unbelief notwithstanding the many mighty works which I have done among them; and as surely as the Lord liveth shall these things be, saith the Lord.

NOTE 9 CHAPTER FOUR .... pg 47

3rd Nephi CHAPTER 23

Jesus approves the words of Isaiah—He commands the people to search the prophets—The words of Samuel the Lamanite concerning the Resurrection are added to their records. About A.D. 34.

1 And now, behold, I say unto you, that ye ought to search these things. Yea, a commandment I give unto you that ye search these things diligently; for great are the words of Isaiah.

2 For surely he spake as touching all things concerning my people which are of the house of Israel; therefore it must needs be that he must speak also to the Gentiles.

3 And all things that he spake have been and shall be, even according to the words which he spake.

4 Therefore give heed to my words; write the things which I have told you; and according to the time and the will of the Father they shall go forth unto the Gentiles.

5 And whosoever will hearken unto my words and repenteth and is baptized, the same shall be saved. Search the prophets, for many there be that testify of these things.

6 And now it came to pass that when Jesus had said these words he said unto them again, after he had expounded all the scriptures unto them which they had received, he said unto them: Behold, other scriptures I would that ye should write, that ye have not.

7 And it came to pass that he said unto Nephi: Bring forth the record which ye have kept.

8 And when Nephi had brought forth the records, and laid them before him, he cast his eyes upon them and said:

9 Verily I say unto you, I commanded my servant Samuel, the Lamanite, that he should testify unto this people, that at the day that the Father should glorify his name in me that there were many saints who should arise from the dead, and should appear unto many, and should minister unto them. And he said unto them: Was it not so?

10 And his disciples answered him and said: Yea, Lord, Samuel did prophesy according to thy words, and they were all fulfilled.

11 And Jesus said unto them: How be it that ye have not written this thing, that many saints did arise and appear unto many and did minister unto them?

12 And it came to pass that Nephi remembered that this thing had not been written.

13 And it came to pass that Jesus commanded that it should be written; therefore it was written according as he commanded.

14 And now it came to pass that when Jesus had expounded all the scriptures in one, which they had written, he commanded them that they should teach the things which he had expounded unto them.

NOTE 10 CHAPTER FOUR............pg 48

3rd Nephi 11

Jesus Christ did show himself unto the people of Nephi, as the multitude were gathered together in the land Bountiful, and did *minister unto them; and on this wise did he show himself unto them. Beginning with chapter 11.*

CHAPTER 11 *The Father testifies of His Beloved Son—Christ appears and proclaims His Atonement—The people feel the wound marks in His hands and feet and side—They cry Hosanna—He sets forth the mode and manner of baptism—The spirit of contention is of the devil—Christ's doctrine is that men should believe and be baptized and receive the Holy Ghost. About A.D. 34.*

1 *And now it came to pass that there were a great multitude gathered together, of the people of Nephi, round about the temple which was in the land Bountiful; and they were marveling and wondering one with another, and were showing one to another the great and marvelous change which had taken place.*

2 *And they were also conversing about this Jesus Christ, of whom the sign had been given concerning his death.*

3 *And it came to pass that while they were thus conversing one with another, they heard a voice as if it came out of heaven; and they cast their eyes round about, for they understood not the voice which they heard; and it was not a harsh voice, neither was it a loud voice; nevertheless, and notwithstanding it being a small voice it did pierce them that did hear to the center, insomuch that there was no part of their frame that it did not cause to quake; yea, it did pierce them to the very soul, and did cause their hearts to burn.*

4 *And it came to pass that again they heard the voice, and they understood it not.*

5 *And again the third time they did hear the voice, and did open their ears to hear it; and their eyes were towards the sound thereof; and they did look steadfastly towards heaven, from whence the sound came.*

6 *And behold, the third time they did understand the voice which they heard; and it said unto them:*

7 Behold my Beloved Son, in whom I am well pleased, in whom I have glorified my name—hear ye him.

8 And it came to pass, as they understood they cast their eyes up again towards heaven; and behold, they saw a Man descending out of heaven; and he was clothed in a white robe; and he came down and stood in the midst of them; and the eyes of the whole multitude were turned upon him, and they durst not open their mouths, even one to another, and wist not what it meant, for they thought it was an angel that had appeared unto them.

9 And it came to pass that he stretched forth his hand and spake unto the people, saying:

10 Behold, I am Jesus Christ, whom the prophets testified shall come into the world.

11 And behold, I am the light and the life of the world; and I have drunk out of that bitter cup which the Father hath given me, and have glorified the Father in taking upon me the sins of the world, in the which I have suffered the will of the Father in all things from the beginning.

12 And it came to pass that when Jesus had spoken these words the whole multitude fell to the earth; for they remembered that it had been prophesied among them that Christ should show himself unto them after his ascension into heaven.

13 And it came to pass that the Lord spake unto them saying:

14 Arise and come forth unto me, that ye may thrust your hands into my side, and also that ye may feel the prints of the nails in my hands and in my feet, that ye may know that I am the God of Israel, and the God of the whole earth, and have been slain for the sins of the world.

15 And it came to pass that the multitude went forth, and thrust their hands into his side, and did feel the prints of the nails in his hands and in his feet; and this they did do, going forth one by one until they had all gone forth, and did see with their eyes and did feel with their hands, and did know of a surety and did bear record, that it was he, of whom it was written by the prophets, that should come.

16 And when they had all gone forth and had witnessed for themselves, they did cry out with one accord, saying:

17 Hosanna! Blessed be the name of the Most High God! And they did fall down at the feet of Jesus, and did worship him.

NOTE 11 CHAPTER FIVE .... pg 59

Book of Mormon, Jacob, Chapter 4:

10 Wherefore, brethren, seek not to counsel the Lord, but to take counsel from his hand. For behold, ye yourselves know that he counseleth in wisdom, and in justice, and in great mercy, over all his works.

11 Wherefore, beloved brethren, be reconciled unto him through the atonement of Christ, his Only Begotten Son, and ye may obtain a resurrection, according to the power of the resurrection which is in Christ, and be presented as the first-fruits of Christ unto God, having faith, and obtained a good hope of glory in him before he manifesteth himself in the flesh.

12 And now, beloved, marvel not that I tell you these things; for why not speak of the atonement of Christ, and attain to a perfect knowledge of him, as to attain to the knowledge of a resurrection and the world to come?

13 Behold, my brethren, he that prophesieth, let him prophesy to the understanding of men; for the Spirit speaketh the truth and lieth not. Wherefore, it speaketh of things as they really are, and of things as they really will be; wherefore, these things are manifested unto us plainly, for the salvation of our souls. But behold, we are not witnesses alone in these things; for God also spake them unto prophets of old.

14 But behold, the Jews were a stiffnecked people; and they despised the words of plainness, and killed the prophets, and sought for things that they could not understand. Wherefore, because of their blindness, which blindness came by looking beyond the mark, they must needs fall; for God hath taken away his plainness from them, and delivered unto them many things which they cannot understand, because they desired it. And because they desired it God hath done it, that they may stumble.

15 And now I, Jacob, am led on by the Spirit unto prophesying; for I perceive by the workings of the Spirit which is in me, that by the stumbling of the Jews they will reject the stone upon which they might build and have safe foundation.

16 But behold, according to the scriptures, this stone shall become the great, and the last, and the only sure foundation, upon which the Jews can build.

NOTE 12 CHAPTER SIX............................ pg 68

Book of Mormon, Alma Chapter 14:

3 And they were also angry with Alma and Amulek; and because they had testified so plainly against their wickedness, they sought to put them away privily.

4 But it came to pass that they did not; but they took them and bound them with strong cords, and took them before the chief judge of the land.

5 And the people went forth and witnessed against them—testifying that they had reviled against the law, and their lawyers and judges of the land, and also of all the people that were in the land; and also testified that there was but one God, and that he should send his Son among the people, but he should not save them; and many such things did the people testify against Alma and Amulek. Now this was done before the chief judge of the land.

6 And it came to pass that Zeezrom was astonished at the words which had been spoken; and he also knew concerning the blindness of the minds, which he had caused among the people by his lying words; and his soul began to be harrowed up under a consciousness of his own guilt; yea, he began to be encircled about by the pains of hell.

7 And it came to pass that he began to cry unto the people, saying: Behold, I am guilty, and these men are spotless before God. And he began to plead for them from that time forth; but they reviled him, saying: Art thou also possessed with the devil? And they spit upon him, and cast him out from among them, and also all those who believed in the words which had been spoken by Alma and Amulek; and they cast them out, and sent men to cast stones at them.

8 And they brought their wives and children together, and whosoever believed or had been taught to believe in the word of God they caused that they should be cast into the fire; and they also brought forth their records which contained the holy scriptures, and cast them into the fire also, that they might be burned and destroyed by fire.

9 And it came to pass that they took Alma and Amulek, and carried them forth to the place of martyrdom, that they might witness the destruction of those who were consumed by fire.

10 And when Amulek saw the pains of the women and children who were consuming in the fire, he also was pained; and he said unto Alma: How can we witness this awful scene? Therefore let us stretch forth our hands, and exercise the power of God which is in us, and save them from the flames.

11 But Alma said unto him: The Spirit constraineth me that I must not stretch forth mine hand; for behold the Lord receiveth them up unto himself, in glory; and he doth suffer that they may do this thing, or that the people may do this thing unto them, according to the hardness of their hearts, that the judgments which he shall

exercise upon them in his wrath may be just; and the blood of the innocent shall stand as a witness against them, yea, and cry mightily against them at the last day.

NOTE 13 CHAPTER SIX............................. pg 69

Book of Mormon, Alma 14:

23 And it came to pass after they had thus suffered for many days, (and it was on the twelfth day, in the tenth month, in the tenth year of the reign of the judges over the people of Nephi) that the chief judge over the land of Ammonihah and many of their teachers and their lawyers went in unto the prison where Alma and Amulek were bound with cords.

24 And the chief judge stood before them, and smote them again, and said unto them: If ye have the power of God deliver yourselves from these bands, and then we will believe that the Lord will destroy this people according to your words.

25 And it came to pass that they all went forth and smote them, saying the same words, even until the last; and when the last had spoken unto them the power of God was upon Alma and Amulek, and they rose and stood upon their feet.

26 And Alma cried, saying: How long shall we suffer these great afflictions, O Lord? O Lord, give us strength according to our faith which is in Christ, even unto deliverance. And they broke the cords with which they were bound; and when the people saw this, they began to flee, for the fear of destruction had come upon them.

27 And it came to pass that so great was their fear that they fell to the earth, and did not obtain the outer door of the prison; and the earth shook mightily, and the walls of the prison were rent in twain, so that they fell to the earth; and the chief judge, and the lawyers, and priests, and teachers, who smote upon Alma and Amulek, were slain by the fall thereof.

28 And Alma and Amulek came forth out of the prison, and they were not hurt; for the Lord had granted unto them power, according to their faith which was in Christ. And they straightway came forth out of the prison; and they were loosed from their bands; and the prison had fallen to the earth, and every soul within the walls thereof, save it were Alma and Amulek, was slain; and they straightway came forth into the city.

29 Now the people having heard a great noise came running together by multitudes to know the cause of it; and when they saw Alma and Amulek coming forth out of the prison, and the walls thereof had fallen to the earth, they were struck with great fear, and fled from the presence of Alma and Amulek even as a goat fleeth with her young from two lions; and thus they did flee from the presence of Alma and Amulek.

Book of Mormon, Alma 25 – 2 But they took their armies and went over into the borders of the land of Zarahemla, and fell upon the people who were in the land of Ammonihah and destroyed them.

NOTE 14 CHAPTER SIX .... *pg 70*

Book of Mormon, Mosiah 24:

8 And now it came to pass that Amulon began to exercise authority over Alma and his brethren, and began to persecute him, and cause that his children should persecute their children.

9 For Amulon knew Alma, that he had been one of the king's priests, and that it was he that believed the words of Abinadi and was driven out before the king, and therefore he was wroth with him; for he was subject to king Laman, yet he exercised authority over them, and put tasks upon them, and put task-masters over them.

10 And it came to pass that so great were their afflictions that they began to cry mightily to God.

11 And Amulon commanded them that they should stop their cries; and he put guards over them to watch them, that whosoever should be found calling upon God should be put to death.

12 And Alma and his people did not raise their voices to the Lord their God, but did pour out their hearts to him; and he did know the thoughts of their hearts.

13 And it came to pass that the voice of the Lord came to them in their afflictions, saying: Lift up your heads and be of good comfort, for I know of the covenant which ye have made unto me; and I will covenant with my people and deliver them out of bondage.

14 And I will also ease the burdens which are put upon your shoulders, that even you cannot feel them upon your backs, even while you are in bondage; and this will I do that ye may stand as witnesses for me hereafter, and that ye may know of a surety that I, the Lord God, do visit my people in their afflictions.

15 And now it came to pass that the burdens which were laid upon Alma and his brethren were made light; yea, the Lord did strengthen them that they could bear up their burdens with ease, and they did submit cheerfully and with patience to all the will of the Lord.

16 And it came to pass that so great was their faith and their patience that the voice of the Lord came unto them again, saying: Be of good comfort, for on the morrow I will deliver you out of bondage.

17 And he said unto Alma: Thou shalt go before this people, and I will go with thee and deliver this people out of bondage.

NOTE 15 CHAPTER EIGHT .... pg 104

Book of Mormon, Moroni Chapter 7

An invitation is given to enter into the rest of the Lord—Pray with real intent—The Spirit of Christ enables men to know good from evil—Satan persuades men to deny Christ and do evil —The prophets manifest the coming of Christ—By faith, miracles are wrought and angels minister—Men should hope for eternal life and cleave unto charity. About A.D. 401–21.

1 And now I, Moroni, write a few of the words of my father Mormon, which he spake concerning faith, hope, and charity; for after this manner did he speak unto the people, as he taught them in the synagogue which they had built for the place of worship.

2 And now I, Mormon, speak unto you, my beloved brethren; and it is by the grace of God the Father, and our Lord Jesus Christ, and his holy will, because of the gift of his calling unto me, that I am permitted to speak unto you at this time.

3 Wherefore, I would speak unto you that are of the church, that are the peaceable followers of Christ, and that have obtained a sufficient hope by which ye can enter into the rest of the Lord, from this time henceforth until ye shall rest with him in heaven.

4 And now my brethren, I judge these things of you because of your peaceable walk with the children of men.

5 For I remember the word of God which saith by their works ye shall know them; for if their works be good, then they are good also.

6 For behold, God hath said a man being evil cannot do that which is good; for if he offereth a gift, or prayeth unto God, except he shall do it with real intent it profiteth him nothing.

7 For behold, it is not counted unto him for righteousness.

8 For behold, if a man being evil giveth a gift, he doeth it grudgingly; wherefore it is counted unto him the same as if he had retained the gift; wherefore he is counted evil before God.

9 And likewise also is it counted evil unto a man, if he shall pray and not with real intent of heart; yea, and it profiteth him nothing, for God receiveth none such.

10 Wherefore, a man being evil cannot do that which is good; neither will he give a good gift.

11 For behold, a bitter fountain cannot bring forth good water; neither can a good fountain bring forth bitter water; wherefore, a man being a servant of the devil cannot follow Christ; and if he follow Christ he cannot be a servant of the devil.

12 Wherefore, all things which are good cometh of God; and that which is evil cometh of the devil; for the devil is an enemy unto God, and fighteth against him continually, and inviteth and enticeth to sin, and to do that which is evil continually.

13 But behold, that which is of God inviteth and enticeth to do good continually; wherefore, every thing which inviteth and enticeth to do good, and to love God, and to serve him, is inspired of God.

14 Wherefore, take heed, my beloved brethren, that ye do not judge that which is evil to be of God, or that which is good and of God to be of the devil.

15 For behold, my brethren, it is given unto you to judge, that ye may know good from evil; and the way to judge is as plain, that ye may know with a perfect knowledge, as the daylight is from the dark night.

16 For behold, the Spirit of Christ is given to every man, that he may know good from evil; wherefore, I show unto you the way to judge; for every thing which inviteth to do good, and to persuade to believe in Christ, is sent forth by the power and gift of Christ; wherefore ye may know with a perfect knowledge it is of God.

17 But whatsoever thing persuadeth men to do evil, and believe not in Christ, and deny him, and serve not God, then ye may know with a perfect knowledge it is of the devil; for after this manner doth the devil work, for he persuadeth no man to do good, no, not one; neither do his angels; neither do they who subject themselves unto him.

18 And now, my brethren, seeing that ye know the light by which ye may judge, which light is the light of Christ, see that ye do not

judge wrongfully; for with that same judgment which ye judge ye shall also be judged.

19 Wherefore, I beseech of you, brethren, that ye should search diligently in the light of Christ that ye may know good from evil; and if ye will lay hold upon every good thing, and condemn it not, ye certainly will be a child of Christ.

20 And now, my brethren, how is it possible that ye can lay hold upon every good thing?

21 And now I come to that faith, of which I said I would speak; and I will tell you the way whereby ye may lay hold on every good thing.

22 For behold, God knowing all things, being from everlasting to everlasting, behold, he sent angels to minister unto the children of men, to make manifest concerning the coming of Christ; and in Christ there should come every good thing.

23 And God also declared unto prophets, by his own mouth, that Christ should come.

24 And behold, there were divers ways that he did manifest things unto the children of men, which were good; and all things which are good cometh of Christ; otherwise men were fallen, and there could no good thing come unto them.

25 Wherefore, by the ministering of angels, and by every word which proceeded forth out of the mouth of God, men began to exercise faith in Christ; and thus by faith, they did lay hold upon every good thing; and thus it was until the coming of Christ.

26 And after that he came men also were saved by faith in his name; and by faith, they become the sons of God. And as surely as Christ liveth he spake these words unto our fathers, saying: Whatsoever thing ye shall ask the Father in my name, which is good, in faith believing that ye shall receive, behold, it shall be done unto you.

27 Wherefore, my beloved brethren, have miracles ceased because Christ hath ascended into heaven, and hath sat down on the right hand of God, to claim of the Father his rights of mercy which he hath upon the children of men?

28 For he hath answered the ends of the law, and he claimeth all those who have faith in him; and they who have faith in him will cleave unto every good thing; wherefore he advocateth the cause of the children of men; and he dwelleth eternally in the heavens.

29 And because he hath done this, my beloved brethren, have miracles ceased? Behold I say unto you, Nay; neither have angels ceased to minister unto the children of men.

30 For behold, they are subject unto him, to minister according to the word of his command, showing themselves unto them of strong faith and a firm mind in every form of godliness.

31 And the office of their ministry is to call men unto repentance, and to fulfil and to do the work of the covenants of the Father, which he hath made unto the children of men, to prepare the way among the children of men, by declaring the word of Christ unto the chosen vessels of the Lord, that they may bear testimony of him.

32 And by so doing, the Lord God prepareth the way that the residue of men may have faith in Christ, that the Holy Ghost may have place in their hearts, according to the power thereof; and after this manner bringeth to pass the Father, the covenants which he hath made unto the children of men.

33 And Christ hath said: If ye will have faith in me ye shall have power to do whatsoever thing is expedient in me.

34 And he hath said: Repent all ye ends of the earth, and come unto me, and be baptized in my name, and have faith in me, that ye may be saved.

35 And now, my beloved brethren, if this be the case that these things are true which I have spoken unto you, and God will show unto you, with power and great glory at the last day, that they are true, and if they are true has the day of miracles ceased?

36 Or have angels ceased to appear unto the children of men? Or has he withheld the power of the Holy Ghost from them? Or will he, so long as time shall last, or the earth shall stand, or there shall be one man upon the face thereof to be saved?

37 Behold I say unto you, Nay; for it is by faith that miracles are wrought; and it is by faith that angels appear and minister unto men; wherefore, if these things have ceased wo be unto the children of men, for it is because of unbelief, and all is vain.

38 For no man can be saved, according to the words of Christ, save they shall have faith in his name; wherefore, if these things have ceased, then has faith ceased also; and awful is the state of man, for they are as though there had been no redemption made.

39 But behold, my beloved brethren, I judge better things of you, for I judge that ye have faith in Christ because of your meekness; for if ye have not faith in him then ye are not fit to be numbered among the people of his church.

40 And again, my beloved brethren, I would speak unto you concerning hope. How is it that ye can attain unto faith, save ye shall have hope?

41 And what is it that ye shall hope for? Behold I say unto you that ye shall have hope through the atonement of Christ and the power of his resurrection, to be raised unto life eternal, and this because of your faith in him according to the promise.

42 Wherefore, if a man have faith he must needs have hope; for without faith there cannot be any hope.

43 And again, behold I say unto you that he cannot have faith and hope, save he shall be meek, and lowly of heart.

44 If so, his faith and hope is vain, for none is acceptable before God, save the meek and lowly in heart; and if a man be meek and lowly in heart, and confesses by the power of the Holy Ghost that Jesus is the Christ, he must needs have charity; for if he have not charity he is nothing; wherefore he must needs have charity.

45 *And charity suffereth long, and is kind, and envieth not, and is not puffed up, seeketh not her own, is not easily provoked, thinketh no evil, and rejoiceth not in iniquity but rejoiceth in the truth, beareth all things, believeth all things, hopeth all things, endureth all things.*

46 *Wherefore, my beloved brethren, if ye have not charity, ye are nothing, for charity never faileth. Wherefore, cleave unto charity, which is the greatest of all, for all things must fail—*

47 *But charity is the pure love of Christ, and it endureth forever; and whoso is found possessed of it at the last day, it shall be well with him.*

48 *Wherefore, my beloved brethren, pray unto the Father with all the energy of heart, that ye may be filled with this love, which he hath bestowed upon all who are true followers of his Son, Jesus Christ; that ye may become the sons of God; that when he shall appear we shall be like him, for we shall see him as he is; that we may have this hope; that we may be purified even as he is pure. Amen.*

NOTE 16 CHAPTER TEN .... pg 124

Book of Mormon, Alma Chapter 32

1 *And it came to pass that they did go forth, and began to preach the word of God unto the people, entering into their synagogues, and into their houses; yea, and even they did preach the word in their streets.*

2 *And it came to pass that after much labor among them, they began to have success among the poor class of people; for behold, they were cast out of the synagogues because of the coarseness of their apparel—*

3 *Therefore they were not permitted to enter into their synagogues to worship God, being esteemed as filthiness; therefore they were poor; yea, they were esteemed by their brethren as dross; therefore*

they were poor as to things of the world; and also they were poor in heart.

4 Now, as Alma was teaching and speaking unto the people upon the hill Onidah, there came a great multitude unto him, who were those of whom we have been speaking, of whom were poor in heart, because of their poverty as to the things of the world.

5 And they came unto Alma; and the one who was the foremost among them said unto him: Behold, what shall these my brethren do, for they are despised of all men because of their poverty, yea, and more especially by our priests; for they have cast us out of our synagogues which we have labored abundantly to build with our own hands; and they have cast us out because of our exceeding poverty; and we have no place to worship our God; and behold, what shall we do?

6 And now when Alma heard this, he turned him about, his face immediately towards him, and he beheld with great joy; for he beheld that their afflictions had truly humbled them, and that they were in a preparation to hear the word.

7 Therefore he did say no more to the other multitude; but he stretched forth his hand, and cried unto those whom he beheld, who were truly penitent, and said unto them:

8 I behold that ye are lowly in heart; and if so, blessed are ye.

9 Behold thy brother hath said, What shall we do?—for we are cast out of our synagogues, that we cannot worship our God.

10 Behold I say unto you, do ye suppose that ye cannot worship God save it be in your synagogues only?

11 And moreover, I would ask, do ye suppose that ye must not worship God only once in a week?

12 I say unto you, it is well that ye are cast out of your synagogues, that ye may be humble, and that ye may learn wisdom; for it is necessary that ye should learn wisdom; for it is because that ye are cast out, that ye are despised of your brethren because of your exceeding poverty, that ye are brought to a lowliness of heart; for ye are necessarily brought to be humble.

13 *And now, because ye are compelled to be humble blessed are ye; for a man sometimes, if he is compelled to be humble, seeketh repentance; and now surely, whosoever repenteth shall find mercy; and he that findeth mercy and endureth to the end the same shall be saved.*

14 *And now, as I said unto you, that because ye were compelled to be humble ye were blessed, do ye not suppose that they are more blessed who truly humble themselves because of the word?*

15 *Yea, he that truly humbleth himself, and repenteth of his sins, and endureth to the end, the same shall be blessed—yea, much more blessed than they who are compelled to be humble because of their exceeding poverty.*

16 *Therefore, blessed are they who humble themselves without being compelled to be humble; or rather, in other words, blessed is he that believeth in the word of God, and is baptized without stubbornness of heart, yea, without being brought to know the word, or even compelled to know, before they will believe.*

17 *Yea, there are many who do say: If thou wilt show unto us a sign from heaven, then we shall know of a surety; then we shall believe.*

18 *Now I ask, is this faith? Behold, I say unto you, Nay; for if a man knoweth a thing he hath no cause to believe, for he knoweth it.*

19 *And now, how much more cursed is he that knoweth the will of God and doeth it not, than he that only believeth, or only hath cause to believe, and falleth into transgression?*

20 *Now of this thing ye must judge. Behold, I say unto you, that it is on the one hand even as it is on the other; and it shall be unto every man according to his work.*

21 *And now as I said concerning faith—faith is not to have a perfect knowledge of things; therefore if ye have faith ye hope for things which are not seen, which are true.*

22 And now, behold, I say unto you, and I would that ye should remember, that God is merciful unto all who believe on his name; therefore he desireth, in the first place, that ye should believe, yea, even on his word.

23 And now, he imparteth his word by angels unto men, yea, not only men but women also. Now this is not all; little children do have words given unto them many times, which confound the wise and the learned.

24 And now, my beloved brethren, as ye have desired to know of me what ye shall do because ye are afflicted and cast out—now I do not desire that ye should suppose that I mean to judge you only according to that which is true—

25 For I do not mean that ye all of you have been compelled to humble yourselves; for I verily believe that there are some among you who would humble themselves, let them be in whatsoever circumstances they might.

26 Now, as I said concerning faith—that it was not a perfect knowledge—even so it is with my words. Ye cannot know of their surety at first, unto perfection, any more than faith is a perfect knowledge.

27 But behold, if ye will awake and arouse your faculties, even to an experiment upon my words, and exercise a particle of faith, yea, even if ye can no more than desire to believe, let this desire work in you, even until ye believe in a manner that ye can give place for a portion of my words.

28 Now, we will compare the word unto a seed. Now, if ye give place, that a seed may be planted in your heart, behold, if it be a true seed, or a good seed, if ye do not cast it out by your unbelief, that ye will resist the Spirit of the Lord, behold, it will begin to swell within your breasts; and when you feel these swelling motions, ye will begin to say within yourselves—It must needs be that this is a good seed, or that the word is good, for it beginneth to enlarge my soul; yea, it beginneth to enlighten my understanding, yea, it beginneth to be delicious to me.

29 Now behold, would not this increase your faith? I say unto you, Yea; nevertheless it hath not grown up to a perfect knowledge.

30 But behold, as the seed swelleth, and sprouteth, and beginneth to grow, then you must needs say that the seed is good; for behold it swelleth, and sprouteth, and beginneth to grow. And now, behold, will not this strengthen your faith? Yea, it will strengthen your faith: for ye will say I know that this is a good seed; for behold it sprouteth and beginneth to grow.

31 And now, behold, are ye sure that this is a good seed? I say unto you, Yea; for every seed bringeth forth unto its own likeness.

32 Therefore, if a seed groweth it is good, but if it groweth not, behold it is not good, therefore it is cast away.

33 And now, behold, because ye have tried the experiment, and planted the seed, and it swelleth and sprouteth, and beginneth to grow, ye must needs know that the seed is good.

34 And now, behold, is your knowledge perfect? Yea, your knowledge is perfect in that thing, and your faith is dormant; and this because you know, for ye know that the word hath swelled your souls, and ye also know that it hath sprouted up, that your understanding doth begin to be enlightened, and your mind doth begin to expand.

35 O then, is not this real? I say unto you, Yea, because it is light; and whatsoever is light, is good, because it is discernible, therefore ye must know that it is good; and now behold, after ye have tasted this light is your knowledge perfect?

36 Behold I say unto you, Nay; neither must ye lay aside your faith, for ye have only exercised your faith to plant the seed that ye might try the experiment to know if the seed was good.

37 And behold, as the tree beginneth to grow, ye will say: Let us nourish it with great care, that it may get root, that it may grow up, and bring forth fruit unto us. And now behold, if ye nourish it with much care it will get root, and grow up, and bring forth fruit.

38 But if ye neglect the tree, and take no thought for its nourishment, behold it will not get any root; and when the heat of the sun cometh and scorcheth it, because it hath no root it withers away, and ye pluck it up and cast it out.

39 Now, this is not because the seed was not good, neither is it because the fruit thereof would not be desirable; but it is because your ground is barren, and ye will not nourish the tree, therefore ye cannot have the fruit thereof.

40 And thus, if ye will not nourish the word, looking forward with an eye of faith to the fruit thereof, ye can never pluck of the fruit of the tree of life.

41 But if ye will nourish the word, yea, nourish the tree as it beginneth to grow, by your faith with great diligence, and with patience, looking forward to the fruit thereof, it shall take root; and behold it shall be a tree springing up unto everlasting life.

42 And because of your diligence and your faith and your patience with the word in nourishing it, that it may take root in you, behold, by and by ye shall pluck the fruit thereof, which is most precious, which is sweet above all that is sweet, and which is white above all that is white, yea, and pure above all that is pure; and ye shall feast upon this fruit even until ye are filled, that ye hunger not, neither shall ye thirst.

43 Then, my brethren, ye shall reap the rewards of your faith, and your diligence, and patience, and long-suffering, waiting for the tree to bring forth fruit unto you.

NOTE 17 CHAPTER TEN .... pg 140

2 Kings 5

1 Now Naaman, captain of the host of the king of Syria, was a great man with his master, and honourable, because by him the Lord had given deliverance unto Syria: he was also a mighty man in valour, but he was a leper.

2 And the Syrians had gone out by companies, and had brought away captive out of the land of Israel a little maid; and she waited on Naaman's wife.

3 And she said unto her mistress, Would God my lord were with the prophet that is in Samaria! for he would recover him of his leprosy.

4 And one went in, and told his lord, saying, Thus and thus said the maid that is of the land of Israel.

5 And the king of Syria said, Go to, go, and I will send a letter unto the king of Israel. And he departed, and took with him ten talents of silver, and six thousand pieces of gold, and ten changes of raiment.

6 And he brought the letter to the king of Israel, saying, Now when this letter is come unto thee, behold, I have therewith sent Naaman my servant to thee, that thou mayest recover him of his leprosy.

7 And it came to pass, when the king of Israel had read the letter, that he rent his clothes, and said, Am I God, to kill and to make alive, that this man doth send unto me to recover a man of his leprosy? wherefore consider, I pray you, and see how he seeketh a quarrel against me.

8 ¶ And it was so, when Elisha the man of God had heard that the king of Israel had rent his clothes, that he sent to the king, saying, Wherefore hast thou rent thy clothes? let him come now to me, and he shall know that there is a prophet in Israel.

9 So Naaman came with his horses and with his chariot, and stood at the door of the house of Elisha.

10 And Elisha sent a messenger unto him, saying, Go and wash in Jordan seven times, and thy flesh shall come again to thee, and thou shalt be clean.

11 But Naaman was wroth, and went away, and said, Behold, I thought, He will surely come out to me, and stand, and call on the name of the Lord his God, and strike his hand over the place, and recover the leper.

12 Are not Abana and Pharpar, rivers of Damascus, better than all the waters of Israel? may I not wash in them, and be clean? So he turned and went away in a rage.

13 And his servants came near, and spake unto him, and said, My father, if the prophet had bid thee do some great thing, wouldest thou not have done it? how much rather then, when he saith to thee, Wash, and be clean?

14 Then went he down, and dipped himself seven times in Jordan, according to the saying of the man of God: and his flesh came again like unto the flesh of a little child, and he was clean.

15 ¶ And he returned to the man of God, he and all his company, and came, and stood before him: and he said, Behold, now I know that there is no God in all the earth, but in Israel: now therefore, I pray thee, take a blessing of thy servant.

16 But he said, As the Lord liveth, before whom I stand, I will receive none. And he urged him to take it; but he refused.

17 And Naaman said, Shall there not then, I pray thee, be given to thy servant two mules' burden of earth? for thy servant will henceforth offer neither burnt offering nor sacrifice unto other gods, but unto the Lord.

18 In this thing the Lord pardon thy servant, that when my master goeth into the house of Rimmon to worship there, and he leaneth on my hand, and I bow myself in the house of Rimmon: when I bow down myself in the house of Rimmon, the Lord pardon thy servant in this thing.

19 And he said unto him, Go in peace. So he departed from him a little way.

20 ¶ But Gehazi, the servant of Elisha the man of God, said, Behold, my master hath spared Naaman this Syrian, in not receiving at his hands that which he brought: but, as the Lord liveth, I will run after him, and take somewhat of him.

21 So Gehazi followed after Naaman. And when Naaman saw him running after him, he lighted down from the chariot to meet him, and said, Is all well?

22 And he said, All is well. My master hath sent me, saying, Behold, even now there be come to me from mount Ephraim two young men of the sons of the prophets: give them, I pray thee, a talent of silver, and two changes of garments.

23 And Naaman said, Be content, take two talents. And he urged him, and bound two talents of silver in two bags, with two changes of garments, and laid them upon two of his servants; and they bare them before him.

24 And when he came to the tower, he took them from their hand, and bestowed them in the house: and he let the men go, and they departed.

25 But he went in, and stood before his master. And Elisha said unto him, Whence comest thou, Gehazi? And he said, Thy servant went no whither.

26 And he said unto him, Went not mine heart with thee, when the man turned again from his chariot to meet thee? Is it a time to receive money, and to receive garments, and oliveyards, and vineyards, and sheep, and oxen, and menservants, and maidservants?

27 The leprosy therefore of Naaman shall cleave unto thee, and unto thy seed for ever. And he went out from his presence a leper as white as snow.

NOTE 18 CHAPTER TEN .... pg 142

Book of Mormon, Moroni Chapter 9

7 And again I speak unto you who deny the revelations of God, and say that they are done away, that there are no revelations, nor prophecies, nor gifts, nor healing, nor speaking with tongues, and the interpretation of tongues;

8 *Behold I say unto you, he that denieth these things knoweth not the gospel of Christ; yea, he has not read the scriptures; if so, he does not understand them.*

9 *For do we not read that God is the same yesterday, today, and forever, and in him there is no variableness neither shadow of changing?*

10 *And now, if ye have imagined up unto yourselves a god who doth vary, and in whom there is shadow of changing, then have ye imagined up unto yourselves a god who is not a God of miracles.*

11 *But behold, I will show unto you a God of miracles, even the God of Abraham, and the God of Isaac, and the God of Jacob; and it is that same God who created the heavens and the earth, and all things that in them are.*

12 *Behold, he created Adam, and by Adam came the fall of man. And because of the fall of man came Jesus Christ, even the Father and the Son; and because of Jesus Christ came the redemption of man.*

13 *And because of the redemption of man, which came by Jesus Christ, they are brought back into the presence of the Lord; yea, this is wherein all men are redeemed, because the death of Christ bringeth to pass the resurrection, which bringeth to pass a redemption from an endless sleep, from which sleep all men shall be awakened by the power of God when the trump shall sound; and they shall come forth, both small and great, and all shall stand before his bar, being redeemed and loosed from this eternal band of death, which death is a temporal death.*

14 *And then cometh the judgment of the Holy One upon them; and then cometh the time that he that is filthy shall be filthy still; and he that is righteous shall be righteous still; he that is happy shall be happy still; and he that is unhappy shall be unhappy still.*

15 *And now, O all ye that have imagined up unto yourselves a god who can do no miracles, I would ask of you, have all these things*

passed, of which I have spoken? Has the end come yet? Behold I say unto you, Nay; and God has not ceased to be a God of miracles.

16 Behold, are not the things that God hath wrought marvelous in our eyes? Yea, and who can comprehend the marvelous works of God?

17 Who shall say that it was not a miracle that by his word the heaven and the earth should be; and by the power of his word man was created of the dust of the earth; and by the power of his word have miracles been wrought?

18 And who shall say that Jesus Christ did not do many mighty miracles? And there were many mighty miracles wrought by the hands of the apostles.

19 And if there were miracles wrought then, why has God ceased to be a God of miracles and yet be an unchangeable Being? And behold, I say unto you he changeth not; if so he would cease to be God; and he ceaseth not to be God, and is a God of miracles.

20 And the reason why he ceaseth to do miracles among the children of men is because that they dwindle in unbelief, and depart from the right way, and know not the God in whom they should trust.

21 Behold, I say unto you that whoso believeth in Christ, doubting nothing, whatsoever he shall ask the Father in the name of Christ it shall be granted him; and this promise is unto all, even unto the ends of the earth.

22 For behold, thus said Jesus Christ, the Son of God, unto his disciples who should tarry, yea, and also to all his disciples, in the hearing of the multitude: Go ye into all the world, and preach the gospel to every creature;

23 And he that believeth and is baptized shall be saved, but he that believeth not shall be damned;

24 And these signs shall follow them that believe—in my name shall they cast out devils; they shall speak with new tongues; they shall take up serpents; and if they drink any deadly thing it shall not hurt them; they shall lay hands on the sick and they shall recover;

25 And whosoever shall believe in my name, doubting nothing, unto him will I confirm all my words, even unto the ends of the earth.

26 And now, behold, who can stand against the works of the Lord? Who can deny his sayings? Who will rise up against the almighty power of the Lord? Who will despise the works of the Lord? Who will despise the children of Christ? Behold, all ye who are despisers of the works of the Lord, for ye shall wonder and perish.

27 O then despise not, and wonder not, but hearken unto the words of the Lord, and ask the Father in the name of Jesus for what things soever ye shall stand in need. Doubt not, but be believing, and begin as in times of old, and come unto the Lord with all your heart, and work out your own salvation with fear and trembling before him.

28 Be wise in the days of your probation; strip yourselves of all uncleanness; ask not, that ye may consume it on your lusts, but ask with a firmness unshaken, that ye will yield to no temptation, but that ye will serve the true and living God.

29 See that ye are not baptized unworthily; see that ye partake not of the sacrament of Christ unworthily; but see that ye do all things in worthiness, and do it in the name of Jesus Christ, the Son of the living God; and if ye do this, and endure to the end, ye will in nowise be cast out.

30 Behold, I speak unto you as though I spake from the dead; for I know that ye shall have my words.

NOTE 19 CHAPTER TWELVE .... pg 171

First Corinthians Chapter 15:

12 Now if Christ be preached that he rose from the dead, how say some among you that there is no resurrection of the dead?

13 But if there be no resurrection of the dead, then is Christ not risen:

14 And if Christ be not risen, then is our preaching vain, and your faith is also vain.

15 Yea, and we are found false witnesses of God; because we have testified of God that he raised up Christ: whom he raised not up, if so be that the dead rise not.

16 For if the dead rise not, then is not Christ raised:

17 And if Christ be not raised, your faith is vain; ye are yet in your sins.

18 Then they also which are fallen asleep in Christ are perished.

19 If in this life only we have hope in Christ, we are of all men most miserable.

20 But now is Christ risen from the dead, and become the first-fruits of them that slept.

21 For since by man came death, by man came also the resurrection of the dead.

22 For as in Adam all die, even so in Christ shall all be made alive.

23 But every man in his own order: Christ the firstfruits; afterward they that are Christ's at his coming.

24 Then cometh the end, when he shall have delivered up the kingdom to God, even the Father; when he shall have put down all rule and all authority and power.

25 For he must reign, till he hath put all enemies under his feet.

26 The last enemy that shall be destroyed is death.

27 For he hath put all things under his feet. But when he saith all things are put under him, it is manifest that he is excepted, which did put all things under him.

28 And when all things shall be subdued unto him, then shall the Son also himself be subject unto him that put all things under him, that God may be all in all.

29 Else what shall they do which are baptized for the dead, if the dead rise not at all? why are they then baptized for the dead?

NOTE 20 CHAPTER THIRTEEN .... *pg 181*

Book of Mormon, 3ʳᵈ Nephi

Jesus Christ did show himself unto the people of Nephi, as the multitude were gathered together in the land Bountiful, and did minister unto them; and on this wise did he show himself unto them. Beginning with chapter 11.

CHAPTER 11

The Father testifies of His Beloved Son—Christ appears and proclaims His Atonement—The people feel the wound marks in His hands and feet and side—They cry Hosanna—He sets forth the mode and manner of baptism—The spirit of contention is of the devil—Christ's doctrine is that men should believe and be baptized and receive the Holy Ghost. About A.D. 34.

1 And now it came to pass that there were a great multitude gathered together, of the people of Nephi, round about the temple which was in the land Bountiful; and they were marveling and wondering one with another, and were showing one to another the great and marvelous change which had taken place.

2 And they were also conversing about this Jesus Christ, of whom the sign had been given concerning his death.

3 And it came to pass that while they were thus conversing one with another, they heard a voice as if it came out of heaven; and they cast their eyes round about, for they understood not the voice which they heard; and it was not a harsh voice, neither was it a loud voice; nevertheless, and notwithstanding it being a small voice it did pierce them that did hear to the center, insomuch that there was no part of their frame that it did not cause to quake; yea, it did pierce them to the very soul, and did cause their hearts to burn.

4 And it came to pass that again they heard the voice, and they understood it not.

5 And again the third time they did hear the voice, and did open their ears to hear it; and their eyes were towards the sound thereof; and they did look steadfastly towards heaven, from whence the sound came.

6 And behold, the third time they did understand the voice which they heard; and it said unto them:

7 Behold my Beloved Son, in whom I am well pleased, in whom I have glorified my name—hear ye him.

8 And it came to pass, as they understood they cast their eyes up again towards heaven; and behold, they saw a Man descending out of heaven; and he was clothed in a white robe; and he came down and stood in the midst of them; and the eyes of the whole multitude were turned upon him, and they durst not open their mouths, even one to another, and wist not what it meant, for they thought it was an angel that had appeared unto them.

9 And it came to pass that he stretched forth his hand and spake unto the people, saying:

10 Behold, I am Jesus Christ, whom the prophets testified shall come into the world.

11 And behold, I am the light and the life of the world; and I have drunk out of that bitter cup which the Father hath given me, and have glorified the Father in taking upon me the sins of the world, in the which I have suffered the will of the Father in all things from the beginning.

12 And it came to pass that when Jesus had spoken these words the whole multitude fell to the earth; for they remembered that it had been prophesied among them that Christ should show himself unto them after his ascension into heaven.

13 And it came to pass that the Lord spake unto them saying:

14 Arise and come forth unto me, that ye may thrust your hands into my side, and also that ye may feel the prints of the nails in my hands and in my feet, that ye may know that I am the God of Israel, and the God of the whole earth, and have been slain for the sins of the world.

15 And it came to pass that the multitude went forth, and thrust their hands into his side, and did feel the prints of the nails in his hands and in his feet; and this they did do, going forth one by one until they had all gone forth, and did see with their eyes and did feel with their hands, and did know of a surety and did bear record, that it was he, of whom it was written by the prophets, that should come.

16 And when they had all gone forth and had witnessed for themselves, they did cry out with one accord, saying:

17 Hosanna! Blessed be the name of the Most High God! And they did fall down at the feet of Jesus, and did worship him.

18 And it came to pass that he spake unto Nephi (for Nephi was among the multitude) and he commanded him that he should come forth.

19 And Nephi arose and went forth, and bowed himself before the Lord and did kiss his feet.

20 And the Lord commanded him that he should arise. And he arose and stood before him.

21 And the Lord said unto him: I give unto you power that ye shall baptize this people when I am again ascended into heaven.

22 And again the Lord called others, and said unto them likewise; and he gave unto them power to baptize. And he said unto them: On this wise shall ye baptize; and there shall be no disputations among you.

23 Verily I say unto you, that whoso repenteth of his sins through your words, and desireth to be baptized in my name, on this wise shall ye baptize them—Behold, ye shall go down and stand in the water, and in my name shall ye baptize them.

24 And now behold, these are the words which ye shall say, calling them by name, saying:

25 Having authority given me of Jesus Christ, I baptize you in the name of the Father, and of the Son, and of the Holy Ghost. Amen.

26 And then shall ye immerse them in the water, and come forth again out of the water.

27 And after this manner shall ye baptize in my name; for behold, verily I say unto you, that the Father, and the Son, and the Holy Ghost are one; and I am in the Father, and the Father in me, and the Father and I are one.

28 And according as I have commanded you thus shall ye baptize. **And there shall be no disputations among you, as there have hitherto been; neither shall there be disputations among you concerning the points of my doctrine, as there have hitherto been.**

29 **For verily, verily I say unto you, he that hath the spirit of contention is not of me, but is of the devil, who is the father of contention, and he stirreth up the hearts of men to contend with anger, one with another. 30 Behold, this is not my doctrine, to stir up the hearts of men with anger, one against another; but this is my doctrine, that such things should be done away.**

NOTE 21 CHAPTER THIRTEEN .... *pg 181*

Book of Mormon, 3rd Nephi Chapter Twelve

Jesus calls and commissions the twelve disciples—He delivers to the Nephites a discourse similar to the Sermon on the Mount—He speaks the Beatitudes—His teachings transcend and take precedence over the law of Moses—Men are commanded to be perfect even as He and His Father are perfect—Compare Matthew 5. About A.D. 34.

1 And it came to pass that when Jesus had spoken these words unto Nephi, and to those who had been called, (now the number of them who had been called, and received power and authority to baptize, was twelve) and behold, he stretched forth his hand unto the multitude, and cried unto them, saying: Blessed are ye if ye shall give heed unto the words of these twelve whom I have chosen from among you to minister unto you, and to be your servants; and unto them I have given power that they may baptize you with water; and after that ye are baptized with water, behold, I will baptize you with fire and with the Holy Ghost; therefore blessed are ye if ye shall believe in me and be baptized, after that ye have seen me and know that I am.

2 And again, more blessed are they who shall believe in your words because that ye shall testify that ye have seen me, and that ye know that I am. Yea, blessed are they who shall believe in your words, and come down into the depths of humility and be baptized, for they shall be visited with fire and with the Holy Ghost, and shall receive a remission of their sins.

3 Yea, blessed are the poor in spirit who come unto me, for theirs is the kingdom of heaven.

4 And again, blessed are all they that mourn, for they shall be comforted.

5 And blessed are the meek, for they shall inherit the earth.

6 And blessed are all they who do hunger and thirst after righteousness, for they shall be filled with the Holy Ghost.

7 And blessed are the merciful, for they shall obtain mercy.

8 And blessed are all the pure in heart, for they shall see God.

9 And blessed are all the peacemakers, for they shall be called the children of God.

10 And blessed are all they who are persecuted for my name's sake, for theirs is the kingdom of heaven.

11 And blessed are ye when men shall revile you and persecute, and shall say all manner of evil against you falsely, for my sake;

12 For ye shall have great joy and be exceedingly glad, for great shall be your reward in heaven; for so persecuted they the prophets who were before you.

13 Verily, verily, I say unto you, I give unto you to be the salt of the earth; but if the salt shall lose its savor wherewith shall the earth be salted? The salt shall be thenceforth good for nothing, but to be cast out and to be trodden under foot of men.

14 Verily, verily, I say unto you, I give unto you to be the light of this people. A city that is set on a hill cannot be hid.

15 Behold, do men light a candle and put it under a bushel? Nay, but on a candlestick, and it giveth light to all that are in the house;

16 Therefore let your light so shine before this people, that they may see your good works and glorify your Father who is in heaven.

17 Think not that I am come to destroy the law or the prophets. I am not come to destroy but to fulfil;

18 For verily I say unto you, one jot nor one tittle hath not passed away from the law, but in me it hath all been fulfilled.

19 And behold, I have given you the law and the commandments of my Father, that ye shall believe in me, and that ye shall repent of your sins, and come unto me with a broken heart and a contrite spirit. Behold, ye have the commandments before you, and the law is fulfilled.

20 Therefore come unto me and be ye saved; for verily I say unto you, that except ye shall keep my commandments, which I have commanded you at this time, ye shall in no case enter into the kingdom of heaven.

21 Ye have heard that it hath been said by them of old time, and it is also written before you, that thou shalt not kill, and whosoever shall kill shall be in danger of the judgment of God;

22 But I say unto you, that whosoever is angry with his brother shall be in danger of his judgment. And whosoever shall say to his brother, Raca, shall be in danger of the council; and whosoever shall say, Thou fool, shall be in danger of hell fire.

23 Therefore, if ye shall come unto me, or shall desire to come unto me, and rememberest that thy brother hath aught against thee—

24 Go thy way unto thy brother, and first be reconciled to thy brother, and then come unto me with full purpose of heart, and I will receive you.

25 Agree with thine adversary quickly while thou art in the way with him, lest at any time he shall get thee, and thou shalt be cast into prison.

26 Verily, verily, I say unto thee, thou shalt by no means come out thence until thou hast paid the uttermost senine. And while ye are in prison can ye pay even one senine? Verily, verily, I say unto you, Nay.

27 Behold, it is written by them of old time, that thou shalt not commit adultery;

28 But I say unto you, that whosoever looketh on a woman, to lust after her, hath committed adultery already in his heart.

29 Behold, I give unto you a commandment, that ye suffer none of these things to enter into your heart;

30 For it is better that ye should deny yourselves of these things, wherein ye will take up your cross, than that ye should be cast into hell.

31 It hath been written, that whosoever shall put away his wife, let him give her a writing of divorcement.

32 Verily, verily, I say unto you, that whosoever shall put away his wife, saving for the cause of fornication, causeth her to commit adultery; and whoso shall marry her who is divorced committeth adultery.

33 And again it is written, thou shalt not forswear thyself, but shalt perform unto the Lord thine oaths;

34 But verily, verily, I say unto you, swear not at all; neither by heaven, for it is God's throne;

35 Nor by the earth, for it is his footstool;

36 Neither shalt thou swear by thy head, because thou canst not make one hair black or white;

37 But let your communication be Yea, yea; Nay, nay; for whatsoever cometh of more than these is evil.

38 And behold, it is written, an eye for an eye, and a tooth for a tooth;

39 But I say unto you, that ye shall not resist evil, but whosoever shall smite thee on thy right cheek, turn to him the other also;

40 And if any man will sue thee at the law and take away thy coat, let him have thy cloak also;

41 And whosoever shall compel thee to go a mile, go with him twain.

42 Give to him that asketh thee, and from him that would borrow of thee turn thou not away.

43 And behold it is written also, that thou shalt love thy neighbor and hate thine enemy;

44 But behold I say unto you, love your enemies, bless them that curse you, do good to them that hate you, and pray for them who despitefully use you and persecute you;

45 That ye may be the children of your Father who is in heaven; for he maketh his sun to rise on the evil and on the good.

46 Therefore those things which were of old time, which were under the law, in me are all fulfilled.

47 Old things are done away, and all things have become new.

48 Therefore I would that ye should be perfect even as I, or your Father who is in heaven is perfect.

Internet Links and Contact Information

THE AUTHOR:
James R. Tate
Tate Bywater
Attorneys at Law 2740 Chain
Bridge Road Vienna, Virginia 22181
Phone: 703-938-5100
Email: jtate@tatebywater.com
Web: www.tatebywater.com

AMERICAN FAMILY ASSOCIATION
Tim Wildmon, *President*
P O Drawer 2440
Tupelo, Mississippi 38803
Phone: 662-844-5036
Email: faq@afa.net
Web: AFA.net - Home
Donor Questions: donorsupport@afa.net

THE CHURCH OF JESUS CHRIST OF LATTER-DAY SAINTS
Web: www.churchofjesuschrist.org
Scriptures: www.churchofjesuschrist.org/study/scriptures
Missionary Department Phone: 801-240-2222
Email: csm-support@ChurchofJesusChrist.org

WA